TEACH FAST

FOCUSED *ADAPTABLE* STRUCTURED TEACHING

Gene Tavernetti, Ed. D.

First published 2022

by John Catt Educational Ltd,
15 Riduna Park, Station Road,
Melton, Woodbridge IP12 1QT
UK
Tel: +44 (0) 1394 389850

4500 140th Ave North,
Suite 101, Clearwater,
FL 33762-3848
US
Tel: +1 561 448 1987

Email: enquiries@johncatt.com
Website: www.johncatt.com

ISBN: 978 1 915261 55 7

Set and designed by John Catt Educational Limited

CONTENTS

ABOUT THE AUTHOR

Gene Tavernetti began his career in education in 1977. He has served as a coach, teacher, counselor, and administrator. He found his true passion when he began to work one-one as an instructional coach. It was during this work that he witnessed the immediate, direct, and positive impact he could have on teachers, administrators, and ultimately student learning.

In 2006, Dr. Tavernetti co-founded Total Educational Systems Support (TESS). Since its founding, TESS, and Gene, have trained and coached thousands of educators in teacher directed instruction emphasizing strategies for engagement, language development, and higher order thinking.

Gene continues to work with selected districts training teachers, coaches, and administrators in reality-based effective instruction.

FOREWORD

Teachers, in recent years, have been tasked with much more than their job title implies. In the cauldron of public education there is constant demand for schools to resolve every social ill or misstep from basic social graces, to gang interventions, to career planning. Schools are asked to feed students and attend to both their physical and mental health. But a critical role of school administrators is to remind everyone that the mission of their schools is to teach.

What is critical in school improvement programs is focus (and continued focus) on the core of our mission – *teaching*. This is not just the general joyous vibe of an abstraction, but an understanding and application of what we know works in terms of pedagogical and discrete skills. To that end, we must remember that teaching is both an art and a science. *Teach FAST: Focused Adaptable Structured Teaching* can be an important building block in any teacher, administrator, or even non-teacher's understanding of this art and science and the fulfillment of that mission.

Most administrators understand, or suspect, that their faculty's grasp of these elements is varied and loosely packed, with wide discrepancies in knowledge of the spectrum of steps needed in the delivery of a comprehensive lesson. Teaching colleges vary widely in terms of what constitutes 'teacher training', especially in their requirements of basic courses, electives, and students' selected majors. Many entry-level teachers, for example, have had little or no instruction on cognitive psychology as applied to learning, i.e. wait time, seat time, the number of new details the brain may absorb at one time, the number of repetitions needed before a bit of information becomes embedded in long-term memory, etc. These, and other, important discoveries of cognitive research are incorporated into the FAST instructional model. If schools are to present the student body with a systematic, systemic, and predictable instructional model, they must focus on staff development and the coalescence of the staff around common experiences – models which will develop a common vocabulary and understanding of critical educational systems and goals.

There is a fundamental precept in human psychology that states, simply, 'everyone wants to succeed'. Teachers, by their very choice to enter the teaching profession, understand this dynamic in humans and want to be part of their student's growth, their success, and their achievements.

The desire to succeed is a human trait that is often overlooked in HR departments, corporate structures, and business relations – but is also an underlying tenant in the process of teaching. After all, our first experiences as living humans are successful learning: nursing, eating, crawling, standing, walking, and communicating – we succeed, and we smile. Teachers witness this dynamic every time a student expresses surprise, a smile, a wave of the raised hand – that glow of pride in understanding and succeeding.

Teach FAST is a guide and a teaching structure that will greatly increase those moments of success in every classroom, and which will help teachers understand more clearly the process of teaching and learning.

Given the ancillary demands that are placed on teachers, this gift of providing efficient, fast learning opportunities is critical. Understanding the science involved in how learning occurs, and the lesson structure that scaffolds logically from past knowledge to new knowledge, is essential if teachers are going to be successful in teaching and students successful in learning.

After spending forty years as a teacher, administrator, and designer of staff development programs Dr. Tavernetti invited me to join his firm, TESS, in 2006. For the next five years I was part of the team doing school intervention work; the training of administrators and teachers, school organization, curriculum development and so forth.

In addition, I had the opportunity to be part of, and witness, the development of the FAST Framework. I saw firsthand its impact on the teaching success of hundreds of teachers. What evolved as the primary focus of our work was instruction (the primary focus of schools), and the FAST Framework.

I would, during our school improvement work, spend more and more time witnessing Dr. Tavernetti's teacher training in learning psychology, coherent lesson delivery, and instruction via the evolving FAST model. Teacher coaching, the task of helping teachers embed the FAST Framework into their pedagogical repertoire, evolved as an essential part of our work.

The development of the framework came over a number of years and with the experience of working with hundreds of teachers and administrators as we moved the model through numerous iterations. Via this coaching, Dr. Tavernetti was given the opportunity to use teacher feedback as the critical link in the development of FAST. I would often hear him say to the teacher, 'This is your classroom – you are the boss. Tell me what you want, what you think.'

And what about coaches and administrators? In my experience, coaches and evaluators are often sent into classrooms with little or no idea what their role actually is – except 'to evaluate' or 'to coach.' Without understanding their respective roles, or the instructional focus of the school, in too many cases they will literally ask the teacher, 'What do you want me to write in my evaluation?' Similar scenarios have led to increased cynicism in teachers ranks about so-called 'in-service.' In fact, in one school we were serving, in our initial meeting with the staff one well-aged teacher asked us, 'OK, what tricks are you going to show us?'

In one large district where we were serving as consultants, it had been decided to reassign forty assistant principals to the role of teacher coaches. Our simple questions to the district were, 'Are they trained in lesson evaluation?' 'Do they know what they're observing?' After considering the cost and the possible damage, the district decided to have us train all the future coaches in the FAST Framework.

The FAST Framework gives site administrators and coaches not only an understanding of instruction, but a valuable tool to help them coach and evaluate the teaching staff. What produces desired results for schools – as with every other challenge in life – is *focus*. Consistency in student achievement is not only predictable by the educational level of their mothers, but also by the consistency of instructional focus within the institution – this is a valuable book for the entire staff, from the teacher to the superintendent.

Teach FAST should be an essential part of any school's intellectual and pedagogical library. It should be revisited every year and be a critical part of all new hire's orientation. It should be followed by coaching to ensure the staff know that this model is to be embedded in the school culture.

Dr. Randall Olson

INTRODUCTION

*'I don't know what you did different
Miss Dannon. But, keep doing it!'*

Excited 4th grader after successfully completing a math lesson.

The FAST Framework provides a structure for delivering lessons more efficiently. These lessons are also more effective because the FAST structure is based on cognitive science that describes how human beings best learn.

The FAST Framework is:

- **F (Focused)**: Focus is a single lesson objective.
- **A (Adaptable)**: A single lesson structure can be used for all content. How to learn efficiently becomes predictable. Predictability allows students to focus on content.
- **S (Structured)**: Based on research that matches how students learn.
- **T (Teaching)**: The teacher is in control of the lesson.

These four features allow instruction to go faster.

Most lessons are way too long and are delivered way too slowly. The purpose of this book is specifically to lay out how to design and deliver focused lessons where students will be successful in a shorter period of time. Shorter lessons mean students can begin practicing sooner, and practice is where learning becomes permanent.

It is not new or startling to learn that effective lessons can be broken down into elements, or components, that make learning easier for students. Effective lessons have a connection to prior learning, an objective, a review, explanations of new concepts, teacher modeling, practice with teacher feedback, and closure. A quick Google search will yield plenty of hits to tell you *what* teachers should do.

The FAST Framework was developed and adapted as an outgrowth of the 5 step or 7 step lesson plan. It uses the same names for the components that are familiar to most teachers, e.g. learning objective, guided practice, independent practice, etc. This was deliberate. I wanted teachers to feel comfortable with the terminology. However, although the names of the components used in the FAST Framework denote similar goals to the 5 step or 7 step lesson plan, the 'how', 'why', and 'when' vary from what teachers may have previously encountered.

Effective lessons have the elements, or components, listed above. Each component is individually important, but it is their interplay that allows lessons to flow. It is the interconnectedness, the cohesiveness, and the interconnections between the components that provide the support and scaffolds for students that move them from ignorance to confidence faster. Each component is important because it is a link of the chain that is the lesson (and a chain is only as strong as its weakest link).

This book is written to assist teachers to design and deliver lessons; the 'what', the 'how', and the 'when' of implementing lesson components in a manner that promotes learning at the optimal times. Knowing what to do as a teacher in the classroom is not enough. Nearly every teacher leaving teacher training programs can tell you what to do. The difference between the best and the rest is they not only know what to include in all the components, but how to deliver lessons in a manner that matches how students learn.[1] The best teachers also know when the most effective times for each component during lessons are.

GUIDED BY RESEARCH ('WHY?')

In the field of education, it is difficult, for ethical and practical reasons, to perform experiments on children in school settings. It has been said that education is research driven, not research based. Much of the research on effective educational instruction and practice is appropriated from the related fields of social psychology and cognitive psychology. This

---

1   No, I do not mean the debunked VAK Learning Styles.

knowledge is synthesized and generalized to create useful structures for teaching.

The information in this book is guided by cognitive research. Why should you care? Cognitive research provides the 'why' that explains the 'what', 'how' and 'when'. Knowing the why is critical for teachers in making decisions during a lesson, e.g. whether to proceed as planned or modify the lesson, whether to pull a small group for immediate intervention or have students begin independent practice. Certain actions, an addition or a deletion, at a particular point in a lesson are driven by the why. Knowing why a lesson is effective helps teachers become critical consumers of commercially produced lessons (such as those found in textbooks), lessons found on-line, or even lessons produced by colleagues.

This book will provide the why – i.e. the research basis for the practices I am recommending – but only tangentially. References and links to research articles, journals, blogs, etc. will be provided, but this book is not intended to be a textbook on research. This book is meant to be a practical guide on designing and delivering instruction. It is a guide that presents the 'what', 'when', 'why', and 'how' of effective instruction and practice.

All that is left is the 'who': you the teacher and your students.

THE GOAL OF THIS BOOK

By the end of this book the reader will be able to design and deliver more efficient and effective first instruction to all students. More effective first instruction means more students are successful. More students being successful means fewer students being remediated.

HOW TO READ THIS BOOK

Reading this book from beginning to end will demonstrate 'how' and 'when' components of lessons are most effective to implement. Each link of the chain, each lesson component, will be discreetly described in the approximate order in which a lesson should be taught.

Reading the book from beginning to end allows the teacher to view the 'whole' of the process, see how components are connected, and how each artfully leads to the next. However, each chapter on individual components is also written to be read or referred to as a stand-alone resource. As such, each chapter contains design and delivery tips, examples, and helpful anecdotes from classrooms that provide additional insight into how to and how not to.

WHAT'S NEW?

Most readers, at some point early in this book, will have one or two common thoughts. First, most readers will think, 'This is just the same old 7 Step Lesson Plan we learned about years ago.' However, they will soon realize that the adaptability of the FAST lesson structure, the cohesion of its components, and the synthesis of learning principles from cognitive science, make the FAST Framework much, much more.

The second thought most readers will have is, 'This may work for some content but not all. What about labs? What about lessons that focus on concepts? What about discovery learning?' If you have those thoughts, don't worry, we will cover all of those issues in the following chapters (see also appendix II on the learning progression; and appendix IV on declarative and procedural lessons). However, before that lets take a look at what you will find in each chapter including its most important details as well as what is new and different from the old 7 step lesson plan.

Chapter 1: Teaching and Learning (Structure vs Strategy)

Big ideas:

- A single lesson structure for all lessons.
- All components are interrelated.
- Reliance on cognitive psychology for *design* and *delivery*.

Design: The FAST Framework is an organizational structure that can be used for teaching all kinds of content. While content may change, how we learn does not, and the structure of lessons does not need to change. All of the lesson components are driven by cognitive science.[2] The science behind each component will be described in order to guide instruction and practice. Understanding what makes a component imperative and effective changes these components from merely something to be

---

2   Although some of the research presented may seem new to teachers and educators, all teachers will be nodding their heads in agreement as they recognize in these descriptions why some classroom procedures or strategies simply do not work.

mechanically 'checked off' by a teacher as completed, to appreciating their importance and degrees of quality.

Delivery: Efficiency is a goal of effective delivery. Lessons should be no longer than students' ability to attend.

Chapter 2: Preview
Big ideas:

- Preview identifies relevant past experiences.
- Connects past experiences to the new concepts in the lesson.
- Past experiences, or prior knowledge, do not have to necessarily be a result of academic experiences.
- Should last no longer than 1-3 minutes.

Design: Preview is usually the first part of the lesson that is delivered to students, but it is often the last component planned. Prior knowledge in the preview should be directly related to the new conceptual knowledge to be presented in the lesson. The preview then becomes the anchor that teachers can return to in order to reinforce new concepts.

Delivery: Teacher addresses question(s) to all students. *Time to deliver the preview should be no more than 1-3 minutes.*

Chapter 3: Learning objective
Big ideas:

- You can only teach one new objective at a time.
- Learning objectives must match independent practice exactly.
- Learning objectives matching independent practice gives direction to the entire lesson.

Design: There should be only one new learning objective in each lesson. This learning objective exactly matches independent practice.

Delivery: Students are referred back to the learning objective during the lesson. *Time to deliver 1-2 minutes.*

Chapter 4: Review
Big ideas:

- Review connects past learned skills to new skills in the lesson.

- Past experiences, or prior knowledge, are a result of academic experiences.
- Students perform the review by answering the teacher's queries.
- Content and context of the review is determined by what skills students will need to be successful in this lesson.

Design: Connected to expert thinking. The review portion of the lesson accesses prior knowledge to help students bridge the gap from their existing knowledge to the new learning in the lesson. Prior knowledge in the review is directly related to concepts and skills previously learned in school.

The review is directly related to the necessary constituent skills that were previously learned. Decisions about what to review are made late in the planning process, after guided practice.

Delivery: The review is asking, not telling. *Time to deliver 2-5 minutes.*

Chapter 5: Key ideas
Big ideas:

- Key ideas is the conceptual part of the lesson.
- Concepts include both declarative and conditional knowledge.
- Concept maps and language frames are introduced.

Design: Conceptual knowledge presented in the key idea portion of the lesson connects to preview, and includes both declarative knowledge and conditional knowledge. Key ideas includes concept maps that visually represent how concepts are related. Also included are language frames that linguistically articulate the relationship of the ideas that are visually represented in the concept maps.

Delivery: Students use language frames to practice articulating concepts using academic language. *Time to deliver 4-12 minutes.*

Chapter 6: Expert thinking
Big ideas:

- Expert thinking is modeling.
- You can't tell students everything you know.

- Not all modeling is created equal.
- Teachers can model how they do procedures.
- Teachers can model how they think about concepts/content.

Design: Connected to review and guided practice. In procedural lessons (lessons in which the skill is new), students are provided with algorithms while the teacher models the steps she uses to solve the problems presented in the lesson. In declarative lessons (lessons in which the concepts are new), students are provided with concept maps that allow the teacher to model how she thinks about the concept.

Delivery: The teacher models two examples. Modeling is uninterrupted by either questions from the students to the teacher or teacher questions to the students. *Time to deliver 2-5 minutes.*

Chapter 7: Guided practice
Big ideas:

- Students are immediately 100% responsible for practicing new skills and concepts.
- Students learn by practicing.
- Effective practice reinforces both concepts and skills.
- The two goals of guided practice are: practice for students and data for teachers.

Design: Connected to expert thinking and independent practice. Three practice problems are selected. The teacher pre-determines how long it should take to do each step.

Delivery: Students are responsible for performing tasks immediately. Feedback is given within seconds of students completing practice tasks. Teacher moves students along quickly as a group. Individual feedback to students is limited. *Time to deliver 5-12 minutes.*

Chapter 8: Closure
Big ideas:

- The teacher's final check for understanding.
- Reconnects the learning objective, key ideas, and expert thinking.

- Recall to relearn: the teacher asks, but the students do the work.

Design: Students respond to teacher questions about the learning objective, key ideas, and expert thinking. Teachers provide the necessary instructive and constructive feedback based on student responses.

Delivery: Closure occurs before independent practice. Students do all the work. *Time to deliver 4-5 minutes.*

Chapter 9: Independent practice
Big ideas:

- Independent practice matches the learning objective exactly.
- In procedural lessons it matches the expert thinking and guided practice.
- In declarative lessons it incorporates content from the expert thinking and guided practice into a cognitively more engaging task.

Design: Independent practice matches the learning objective exactly. There is independent practice at the end of every lesson.

Delivery: Students should be able to work independently. *Time to deliver 5 to 12 minutes.*

Chapter 10: Wrap up
A final recap of the components.

Appendices
There are several appendices included to provide background and support in implementing the design and delivery of FAST Framework Lessons. These additional materials include:

- Concept maps and language frames.
- Learning progression.
- Classroom management and procedures.
- Declarative and procedural lessons.

CHAPTER 1
TEACHING AND LEARNING (STRUCTURE *VS* STRATEGY)

Big ideas in teaching and learning:

- Reasons why lessons are not successful.
- Student limitations.
- Leveraging limitations.
- FAST Framework.

THE FAST FRAMEWORK: WHY IS IT IMPORTANT?

Why lessons are not successful #1

After observing thousands of lessons in high achieving schools, low achieving schools, and schools somewhere in between, the most frequently observed reason lessons were not successful was that the teacher attempted to teach too much. How is success judged? By a very simple metric. More than 90% of students should be able to successfully complete independent practice.

The cost of attempting to teach too much in one lesson is dear. The obvious result, as noted above, is that considerably fewer students are able to successfully complete independent practice. Although that is bad, of more consequence is the damage to students beyond the individual lesson. A result of attempting to cram too much content into a single lesson is that many students become frustrated, overwhelmed, and just plain give up. When a teacher attempts to teach more than students can learn, and day after day students cannot keep up, they begin to believe that there is something wrong with them.[3] Ironically, when too much content is crammed into a single lesson many students end up learning less than if the teacher actually presented less.

Being successful in a lesson when too much content is presented is a problem that is not limited to struggling students. The impact of too much content is most evident in struggling students. However, the reality is that all students, in fact, all human beings, have limitations with respect to the amount of new content which they can attend to and retain during a defined learning episode. Limitations that exist in humans outside of the classroom will also manifest within the classroom.[4]

In any given day, hour, or even moment, human beings are bombarded with sensory stimuli. Horns honk. People sneeze. Music plays. A workspace is messy. Someone at the next table is speaking loudly on a cell phone. This continuous data stream can be overwhelming. The brain must do something to mitigate this great volume of sensory data. Our brain is constantly evaluating and categorizing this sensory data and then integrates it into existing schema or mental models based on prior knowledge and experience. By organizing data into existing categories, we are not continuously surprised by familiar data.

Organization of stimuli also allows new information to be tested quickly. Without conscious effort we ask ourselves, 'Have I encountered this information before? How does this new data compare and contrast with information previously learned? Is this situation similar to others I have encountered?'

Even after utilizing existing schema to maximize the amount of data being received, the brain may still need to protect itself from sensory overload. One way this is achieved is through conscious focus. For example, if an individual is walking down a busy city street looking for a particular address, she may not notice people in her environment that would distract

---

3   Although this book does not directly address the affective impact of instruction, it is impossible to divorce affect from instruction in the classroom.

4   Many have described school as not being the 'real world.' School is very much the real world. Students use the very same senses and emotions to process school as they use to process their other experiences.

her from her search. Or an individual may be so focused on a conversation she is having on her cell phone that she does not notice that she is crossing the street directly into oncoming traffic.

Just as the brain filters sensory data in the natural world, students' brains are continuously making decisions about data received during a learning episode in a classroom. Students are unconsciously asking themselves, 'What is important? How does this relate to other experiences I have had? Do I already know how to do something similar to this?' If students are trained in how to learn, these questions will form an organizational structure that will help them learn new content more easily.

If students cannot make sense of the content in relation to something they already know or have experienced, they will have a difficult time focusing on what is new. The result is the aforementioned feelings of frustration, overload, and being overwhelmed. One way in which our brains mitigate sensory overload is to be constantly deciding, 'That data is not important. I am not paying attention to that.'

Cognitive load theory

To help us understand why too much content in any one lesson is detrimental to student learning, it is important to introduce cognitive load theory.[5] According to this approach there are three factors that contribute to a person's ability to learn new content during a lesson.[6]

1. **Intrinsic load** – the complexity of the information and the experience of the learner. This is the required load in remembering and learning.

---

5   I have taken many liberties with my descriptions of the cognitive science supporting the FAST Framework. The purpose of this book is to synthesize disparate scientific facts that explain how we learn, and to create a lesson structure that is easily understood yet grounded in research, rather than give a detailed account of the current state of cognitive science.

6   For an accessible discussion of these three parts see Jamies Thomas (2019), 'The Good, The Bad and The (Can Be) Ugly: The Three Parts of Cognitive Load', Available at, https://mcdreeamiemusings.com/blog/2019/10/15/the-good-the-bad-and-the-can-be-ugly-the-three-parts-of-cognitive-load.

2. **Germane load** – the good load in learning. The necessary load shouldered by working memory to construct schemas and transfer material to long-term memory.

3. **Extraneous load** – the bad or unnecessary load in learning. It does not contribute to retention of material. Instructional practices either minimize or maximize extraneous load.[7]

Through thoughtful lesson design a teacher can guide students to focus on particular incoming stimuli over other competing stimuli in the lesson. This is achieved by offering up cues to students that allow them to make connections from material to prior experiences. Metaphorically, the teacher is yelling, 'Over here! Over here! This is very similar to something you already know.'

Connecting new content to prior learning reduces stimuli interference, and it brings meaning to that new content. It is similar to the excitement you feel when you are traveling abroad and you meet someone who is also from the United States. Even though you know nothing about that person you have just enough in common to keep you focused on your commonality for at least a brief time.

Why lessons are not successful #2

Although teaching too much content is the most frequently observed teacher behavior limiting student success, the second is teachers' low expectations of their students performance during the lesson.

It is extremely likely that the above statement ('teachers have low expectations'), would be vigorously challenged by most teachers. In fact, my ears are burning right now as readers vehemently disagree. Ask any teacher, 'Do you have high expectations for your students?' Their answer will be, 'Of course I do!' In fact, I am certain 100% of current teachers proclaimed their high expectations during their initial hiring interview.

Although most teachers would profess high expectations, it is clear that these have not been operationalized into their lessons. It is one thing

---

7   How does extraneous load manifest in the classroom? Many times it is observed when teachers attempt to make lessons so engaging the students are not able to distinguish what is essential from what is just interesting or entertaining. Often in primary grades, teachers make lessons so cute students get distracted.

to proclaim high expectations. It is quite another to design lessons that allow, and even require, students to demonstrate higher levels of cognitive engagement and achievement.

Without specific training in how to maximize instructional effectiveness and efficiency as described in this book, it is extremely difficult to convince teachers that their students are capable of much more. Why? The teachers have tons of evidence that demonstrates their students have not performed at high levels in the past.

At first blush these two common mistakes, teaching too much and having low expectations, seem contradictory. Isn't teaching less during a lesson a demonstration of lowered expectations? The answer is no.

How do lowered expectations manifest? They are directly related to teaching too much content. When a teacher designs a lesson with too much content, they either intuitively or consciously know there is too much content for a student to learn in one lesson. In observations and discussions with classroom teachers this commonly occurs while beginning new units. When asked what the goal for the day is when beginning a new unit, the teacher will frequently respond, 'I just want to introduce the material to the students.'[8] 'That is great,' I will respond. 'But what do you want the students to know at the end of the lesson?'

Teaching less during a lesson is simply the acknowledgement of a biological and neurological reality. Raising expectations is the acknowledgment that if students are taught using well designed and delivered lessons they are capable of learning much more during a single lesson and ultimately much more over the course of a unit and beyond.

UNDERSTANDING STUDENT LIMITATIONS

The way a teacher limits the amount of new content in a lesson should match how human beings process their experiences in the natural world. In order to avoid the two most common mistakes in lesson design, teachers must understand some functional limitations of all students in the processing of information.

---

8   With my lips sealed, I imagine this teacher in front of the classroom saying, 'Class, this is the Pythagorean Theorem. Pythagorean Theorem, this is the class.'

These limitations are (1) the amount of information we can hold and process in working memory, and (2) the amount of time we can attend (i.e. give our attention).

Working memory

Working memory is where 'thinking' occurs. All students learn new concepts and skills relative to prior knowledge and/or experience in the environment. When students are learning new concepts and skills, teachers must be aware that students' working memories, by necessity, will be occupied by these new concepts and skills as well as prior knowledge drawn from long term memory. When designing lessons teachers must account for the new concepts and skills as well as previously learned requisite skills. A working memory that is overloaded will greatly inhibit the ability of students to learn and practice new concepts and skills.

Information held in working memory is very short term – the duration of time that new content is being synthesized. A synthesis of new and prior knowledge is necessary to learn a new concept or skill in a new context. For example, learning the concept of an extended metaphor (new concept) requires both an understanding of the concept of a metaphor (prior knowledge) and integrating that knowledge into a new context.

Overloading the working memory – attempting to have students engage in new processes that are beyond what they are currently capable of – will lead to frustration.

What is the capacity of the working memory? The most frequently cited research is based George Miller's work on 'one-dimensional memory', i.e. memorizing a string of numbers, or memorizing a number of tones. Miller's research yielded the result that working memory was limited in adults to the 'magic number' 7. According to this research, adults were found to be able to hold 7 items, plus or minus 2, in working memory.[9]

Building on this idea, various researchers identify a range of other numbers of 'chunks' of information that can be held in working memory, i.e. there are several 'magic numbers'. However, most studies identify 3-5

---

9   Memorizing numbers or tones is not nearly as sophisticated as learning complex concepts or skills. It is evident teachers must consider the cognitive load in each lesson.

chunks, plus or minus two, for adults. This limitation will vary based on the age of the learner.

What is a 'chunk' of information? A 'chunk' is defined as:

> ... a familiar collection of more elementary units that have been inter-associated and stored in memory repeatedly and act as a coherent, integrated group when retrieved.[10]

Whether the magic number is 2 chunks, 3 chunks, 4 chunks, 5 chunks, 6 chunks, or even 7 chunks may be interesting in terms of cognitive science, but is not actually relevant in a practical sense. What is relevant is for teachers to realize that whatever the magic number actually is, it is very small. In fact, when designing a lesson, teachers cannot go wrong erring on the low side.

It is evident in this definition that a chunk of information is variable based on the student. An example may illustrate why this variability occurs. Imagine a 4th grader is asked to solve a story problem in math class that involves the use of long division.[11] To solve such a problem a student must be able to perform the following tasks (and possibly more):

- Decode the words in the story problem.
- Understand the key elements of the story.
- Identify the conditions that determine division is the preferred method to solve the problem.
- Write the equation.
- Perform long division.

A student who can proficiently perform the above tasks with fluency and near automaticity may only need to hold two to four chunks of information in their working memory while solving the story problem. A student who is a proficient reader will have collapsed the first two skills, (1) decoding

---

10   Tulving, E. & Craik, F. (2000) *The Oxford Handbook of Memory*. Oxford: Oxford University Press, p. 12.

11   The use of long division to solve story problems of the type that asks 'How many groups of _____ are there?' is never actually necessary – there are always alternative algorithms that could be used. For example, one might use repeated subtraction. For purposes of this example imagine that long division is the mathematical algorithm that is expected to be practiced.

and (2) understanding the key elements of the story, into one single chunk that may be called simply 'reading.' The proficient math student may also collapse (4) write the equation, and (5) perform long division into a single chunk.

On the other hand, for a student who is not proficient in any one of the above identified skills, the germane cognitive load will not be two to four chunks but could be many many more. For example, a student who is not a proficient reader may use all his cognitive capacity just to decode the story problem using phonetic strategies, and may never even get to the division problem. Or, the student may reach the limit of his working memory attempting to recall the discrete steps involved in solving long division problems.

The expert teacher understands the limitations of her students and provides appropriate scaffolding to mitigate the problem posed by limitations of working memory. This can be done in various ways such as proper chunking, providing resources to reduce cognitive load, and/or limiting tasks (these scaffolds will be discussed in the lesson component chapters). None of these issues preclude all students from engaging in rigorous lessons.

Attention span

The brain did not evolve to receive continuous input. In fact, the amount of time we can attend to new information is very limited. Many teachers have protested the validity of this claim. As evidence to dispute the claim, teachers cite the amount of time students can attend to video games or other activities that they enjoy. Although it is true that students can attend to games or other activities for extended periods of time, they are not learning new information.[12]

Time limitations on attention have popularly been expressed in two ways. The first is a time limit based on the age of the student. The time limit is approximately 1 minute per year of age. For example, the average 5-year-old can attend for approximately 5 minutes, a 6 year old for approximately 6 minutes, a 10 year old for 10 minutes, etc. This pattern holds up to

---

12 Learning happens in two stages: instruction and practice. The limitations of time described above pertain to instruction of new content.

about age eighteen when it tops out. The second limit is a flat 10-minute rule. Regardless of age, instructional input should not last longer than 10 minutes. In either case, the amount of time is an approximate average.[13]

What is interesting about these limitations is that the mode of presentation is irrelevant. As teachers begin to use more varied technologies to deliver content, it is easy for them to fall into the trap of believing that technology will trump physiology. However, this time limitation holds regardless of the mode of delivery: whether the content is presented orally through some type of lecture, through a multimedia presentation, or some combination of the two. Do not fall into the extraneous load trap by using the latest technological bells and whistles on the latest platforms as an attempt to stretch students' attention limitations.

As with the number of chunks held in working memory, the exact number of minutes is irrelevant to the classroom teacher. What is relevant is that a limitation exists. Remember the proverb 'Less is more!'

MITIGATING LIMITATIONS: OPTIMAL WINDOWS OF LEARNING (OWLS)

The limitations described above – the number of chunks of information students can hold in working memory, and the amount of time students can attend to new information – provide guidance for how teachers should use the FAST Framework to structure a lesson (see component descriptions section below). It is logical that if students have a limited ability to attend to information, then teachers should present the most important information (the new information), at the beginning of the lesson.

This commonsense approach of teaching the most important content at the beginning of the lesson, is backed by multiple studies.[14] For example, Murdoch (1962) found that retention of new information was highest at the beginning of a learning episode.[15] The second highest retention period

---

13 How is that for using two weasel words in the same sentence?

14 For a summary see, McLeod, S. A. (2008) 'Serial position effect'. *Simply Psychology*. Available at: www.simplypsychology.org/primacy-recency.htm.

15 Murdock, B. B. (1962) 'The serial position effect of free recall'. *Journal of Experimental Psychology*, 64 (5), pp. 482–488.

is during the end of the learning episode. The theory based on this body of research is called Primacy-Recency. Stated plainly, during a learning episode, a student will remember any information presented early in the lesson best (Primacy), and what comes last second best (Recency).[16]

Synthesizing these two concepts – i.e. Primacy-Recency and the limitation of the amount of time students can attend – can guide teachers in design and delivery. The FAST Framework supports teachers in identifying the optimal times for instruction and practice: these are called Optimal Windows for Learning, or OWLs.

The two OWLs are at the beginning and the end of the learning episode. The lesson components that optimally comprise OWL 1 are *key ideas* and *expert thinking*. These are the components where new content is presented and modeled. The lesson components that optimally comprise OWL 2 are *closure* and *independent practice*. These are the components where new content is retrieved from memory and practiced.

The term 'optimally' is used above because effective instruction and practice does not occur in those time frames by accident. Teachers must be conscious of the OWLs in both the design and delivery of lessons. To do anything less is attempting to defy how students naturally learn.

THE FAST FRAMEWORK

FAST is an acronym for Focused Adaptable Structured Teaching. Before we examine and describe each component in the FAST Framework, let us briefly examine the notion of a single unifying structure and how it addresses and mitigates the limitations described above by helping teachers manage cognitive load in lessons.

> **Focused**: Focus helps teachers determine what to include in a lesson (i.e. intrinsic and germane cognitive load), as well as what not to include (i.e. extraneous cognitive load).

> **Adaptable**: How students learn new content does not change based on the type of learning goal. A teacher may employ different strategies for presenting new information, but the strategies are employed

---

16　It is common to encounter research just mentioning Primacy, remembering best what comes first.

within the FAST Framework. The FAST Framework can be adapted for different learning goals. A single framework helps students become more 'meta' about their learning.

Structured: When teachers understand that there is a single structure for effective lesson design, designing lessons becomes easier because there are many decisions that do not have to be made fresh each time.[17]

The FAST Framework is the structure. Effective instruction will include the components of preview, learning objective, review, key ideas (concepts), expert thinking (modeling), guided practice, closure, and independent practice.[18]

Structure is the roadmap that keeps lessons moving on time.

Teaching: Each component is related to the others to create coherent lessons. To reiterate, lesson coherence is critical to reducing the cognitive load of a lesson by minimizing extraneous cognitive load. Controlling cognitive load allows more students to be successful in any particular lesson.

COMPONENT DESCRIPTIONS

Lets look at a brief overview of the FAST Framework and consider each of its lesson components in turn (they will all be discussed in greater detail in the following chapters).

---

17 A characteristics of experts is that when facing a new problem their universe of possible solutions is much more limited than that of a novice. The novice must work much harder because she does not know what will not work.

18 Much of the literature on group learning, discovery learning, project learning or other methods in which students are to intuit concepts and knowledge confuse effective instruction with practice.

TESS
TOTAL EDUCATIONAL SYSTEMS SUPPORT

FAST Framework

Grade: _____
Standard: _____

GUIDING QUESTION: Is this lesson *declarative* (something to know)
or *procedural* (something to do)?

RETENTION

NEW LEARNING

| OWL 1 | | OWL 2 |
| Inline Synthesis | |

TIME

	LESSON COMPONENT	TEACHER ACTION	LANGUAGE STRATEGY / EDU PROTOCOL	CHECK FOR UNDERSTANDING
INTRODUCTION TO LESSON	**PREVIEW** Access prior knowledge and/or provide relevance			
	LEARNING OBJECTIVE Deconstructed standard			
	REVIEW Sub-skills necessary for **this** lesson			
TEACH – (Provide Input) OWL 1	**KEY IDEAS** Concept Map Definitions Rules Conditions			Include: Use of Language Frames
	EXPERT THINKING Steps/ Concept Map			
INLINE SYNTHESIS	**GUIDED PRACTICE/ GRADUAL RELEASE** Teacher gradually releases control to student			Include: Collaborative Strategies
END OF LINE SYNTHESIS - OWL 2	**CLOSURE** Teacher's final check for understanding			
	INDEPENDENT PRACTICE Matches learning objective			

© 2022 Gene Tavernetti, Frank Rodriguez

Preview

The purpose of the preview is to connect prior conceptual knowledge to new concepts in the lesson.[19] Students possess prior conceptual knowledge that relates to what they have experienced in their lives. The teacher presents the students with a question or problem. The aim is to prompt the students to make the connection themselves rather than the teacher simply telling the students how the new lesson relates to experiences those students may have had.

For example, imagine that the learning objective for a kindergarten class is to distinguish between 'am' and 'pm'. As a preview question, the teacher may ask students, 'What activities do you perform after you wake up in the morning?' And, also, 'What activities do you perform before you go to sleep at night?' Notice that the questions are paired conceptually to something universal to all the students. They would be able to respond to these questions; not because of any prior lesson, but merely because they have been alive for 5 or 6 years and they all sleep.

Preview is usually the first lesson component that is delivered, but it is the last in the planning process. The reason for this is simple. One of the strengths of the FAST Framework is the 'tightness', i.e. the cohesion of the lesson and the interconnectedness of its components. If the two questions mentioned above were to be asked in the preview, then the teacher would explain the concepts of am and pm by using activities students perform at different times of the day. The activities that are initially identified by students become an anchor for the new concepts.

Learning objective

The learning objective provides the target for the lesson. This learning objective should be clear and use academic language appropriate for the grade level. Without a learning objective the teacher has no focus and students do not know what information most deserves their attention. Learning objectives will identify the concepts and skills that will be taught, or will be necessary to be successful in the independent practice. For example, if students will interpret metaphors in a poem, then the concept

---

19 Many times in math lessons the review and preview can be combined by setting problems in which the students not only perform the skill but the concept is embedded. This will be explained further in the chapters on review and preview.

is metaphors, and the skill is to interpret. Concepts in learning objectives will be a noun, skills will be a verb.

Review

The review component is important because we all build new knowledge by connecting new material to prior knowledge. Learning requires students to actively engage with both. In the common usage of the term review we imagine a teacher repeating for students something that was previously taught. Oh, if it were only that simple! If all a teacher needed to do was to tell students the information one more time, books like this one would not exist.

The purpose of the review is not to inform students what the critical prior learning was. The purpose of the review is to prompt the students' recall of concepts and skills from long-term memory. Being told, or being reminded, of a fact or skill is passive and does not require students to truly engage with the information. On the other hand, if students are required to *actively* solve a problem or respond to a factual question, then students are forced to recall information stored in long-term memory.

When a teacher prompts students during review two outcomes will result. Firstly, students will recall the prior learning that is critical for the new lesson and strengthen their neural pathways to that memory. Secondly, the teacher will identify which students did not recall the information. This data will then guide the teacher in how to provide appropriate scaffolding for those students to allow them to participate and succeed in the lesson.

Key ideas

Key ideas are the new concepts and pertinent facts of the lesson. The key ideas include both declarative knowledge and conditional knowledge. Declarative knowledge is the 'what' of the lesson. Declarative knowledge would also include how the new concept relates to previously learned concepts. Conditional knowledge explains 'when' students will encounter the content and when application of their newly learned skills is appropriate. In other words, under what conditions does this concept apply?

If a teacher is not personally clear on the key ideas, and does not understand the concepts critical to the lesson, then that teacher cannot teach this lesson successfully.

Key ideas are presented before expert thinking, or modeling. Before teachers demonstrate 'how', they must teach 'what'. If a teacher models for students without first developing an understanding of underlying concepts, then that teacher is not fostering a deep understanding of the content. It is as if students are learning a trick, not developing problem solving skills.

'Is this where we do the vocabulary?' many teachers ask. The answer is yes, but in order to understand key ideas and concepts students need much more than definitions. Students should be provided with a definition, but that definition must be in context. In addition to definitions students need examples and non-examples. Teachers must be extremely discriminating when providing definitions and examples. Clear defenitions and examples of key ideas are so critical to understanding that it cannot be left to students to find them (and finding defenitions should not be assigned as a task for the same reason).

Expert thinking

Expert thinking (i.e. modeling) is the 'how to' part of the lesson.[20] Expert thinking is expressed differently in a declarative lesson than in a procedural lesson.[21] In declarative lessons the teacher models two examples of how she thinks about a concept by using a concept map. In procedural lessons the teacher models two examples of how she solves a problem by using a step-by-step procedure.

Embedded in expert thinking should be the concepts from the key ideas component of the lesson. Each repetition of a task assigned as guided or independent practice should reinforce the key ideas of the lesson. For example, during a subtraction lesson in which the objective is to subtract a one-digit number from a two-digit number, the following are a few sample problems:

---

20   To avoid confusion the term 'modeling' will be used throughout this chapter to identify what the teacher is doing while explaining expert thinking.

21   See appendix IV. The differences between these two lesson types will be more fully discussed in the succeeding chapters.

$12 - 3 =$ _____

$37 - 8 =$ _____

$97 - 6 =$ _____

The new concept in this example lesson is regrouping when necessary. The teacher would demonstrate how tens and ones can be regrouped differently to create equivalent values. They would also emphasize the condition that would trigger the need to regroup when using conventional algorithms. Instruction, practice, and checking for understanding of those concepts would take place during the review and key ideas components of the lesson before the teacher explains her expert thinking.

The procedure for the solving the above problems would be:

1. Analyze.
2. Regroup if necessary.
3. Subtract.
4. Is answer reasonable?

During her expert thinking the teacher would detail her thoughts regarding her decision to regroup or not to regroup. She would also include her thoughts about creating equivalent expressions (not changing values) when regrouping. By including those expert thoughts, the teacher is continuously reinforcing both declarative and conditional concepts embedded in each repetition.

In other words, key ideas are operationalized in the procedure that is being modeled. The importance of key ideas should be demonstrated and acknowledged each time the teacher models a problem as well as each time a student solves a problem during the guided practice that is described below.

Guided practice

There are two goals of guided practice: one for the student and one for the teacher. The goal for students is to learn the step-by-step procedure that will be used to operationalize the key ideas. The goal for the teacher is to gather data to determine which students are able to continue practicing independently, and which students need immediate in-class intervention.

Guided practice provides the first opportunity for students to practice solving problems with feedback and support from the teacher. Guided practice provides students with the opportunity to try for themselves what the teacher has just modeled during her expert thinking. During guided practice in procedural lessons, the teacher will facilitate practice of the step-by-step procedure by directing the students to perform certain steps. The teacher then checks each student to provide constructive and instructive feedback to the class.

As previously stated, the design and names of components in the FAST Framework were purposely chosen to provide familiarity. When teachers are first introduced to the FAST Framework, many naturally compare its components with other instructional models that have an 'I do, we do, and you do' format. For many teachers, guided practice is equated with the 'we do' component of other direct instruction models, where the teacher and the students will do problems together. However, one of the most important differences between the delivery of FAST Framework lessons and those of other models occurs during guided practice. In the FAST Framework students *immediately* begin solving problems by themselves following the expert thinking component. What makes this possible is the manner in which the guided practice is structured.

Are students ready to attempt to solve problems on their own after watching their teacher model only two problems? The answer is yes, no, and I don't know. For teachers to accomplish one of the goals of guided practice – determining which students need additional support – teachers must quickly collect student performance data.

This chapter began with the two most commonly observed reasons why lessons are not successful. One of those reasons was low expectations. When teachers are first introduced to guided practice as it is described above many do not believe that it is possible for their students to begin to work immediately. These teachers then sometimes undermine the lesson structure by providing clues, cues, or even actual answers instead of allowing students to succeed on their own. Not all students will succeed initially. That is what practice is for.

Closure

Closure is probably the most important lesson component that is most commonly not included in lessons. Why is closure important?[22] It provides students with another opportunity to recall information and to relearn it during a high retention time (OWL 2). Closure is the final check for understanding before the teacher decides to either release students to independent practice or to pull a group of students for immediate intervention.

Teachers confuse *closure*, which is the teacher asking the students to respond to questions and problems, with the teacher simply providing a *summary* of what was done. Like the review component of the lesson, the teacher is not *telling*, she is *asking* students.

Designing closure for lessons is not complicated. Questions and prompts should cover three components from the lesson: the learning objective, key ideas, and expert thinking. Using questions that allow data to be collected in specific periods of the lesson helps the teacher be more efficient during immediate in-class interventions.

Independent practice

Independent practice also occurs in OWL 2, a high retention time. Immediate independent practice allows the students to begin to move new content to long-term memory through sufficient practice repetitions.

DESIGN TIPS

Tip #1. Use the planning order

You may have heard the phrase, 'plan with the end in mind.' That is the idea behind the order in which you should plan a lesson using the FAST Framework. The order you deliver a lesson is the order in which the components are displayed on the FAST Framework document (see p. 28). The recommended planning order is very different.

Any endeavor that has a clear endpoint, or goal, will more easily maintain focus. With that in mind, here is the recommended order to design lessons:

---

22   See chapter 7.

- Learning objective.
- Independent practice.
- Key ideas.
- Expert thinking (modeling).
- Guided practice.
- Review.
- Closure.
- Preview.

This planning order is more efficient because what happens in the final four components is dependent upon what happens in the first four components. For example, in the chapters that follow, you will learn that what ultimately needs to be reviewed will be determined by how new content is modeled.[23]

Tip #2. Use limitations help make decisions
When I designed my first lesson, I began to list all things I wanted to include. I had one great idea after another. My students were going to love it!

By the time I was done listing all wonderful things that would be included in the key ideas I realized it would take more than an hour just for key ideas. Knowing I only had about eight minutes to present everything the students needed to be successful in doing independent practice helped me decide what really needed to be in the lesson.

DELIVERY TIPS

Tip #1. Use the delivery order
Lessons are delivered in the approxomite order in which the components have been presented:

- Preview: an 'anchor' that connects prior known concepts to new concept.

---

23   This planning order is recommended for all teachers. With experience teachers will develop their own ideas about the order of planning and running specific lessons. That is fine – when it is fine – on the other hand, if you are having difficulty designing a lesson, you can always go back to the old standby.

- Learning objective: the focus and 'target' of the new lesson.
- Review: the students recall and connect the known constituent skills critical to the new lesson.
- Key ideas: concepts and conditions – the 'what' and 'when' of the lesson.
- Expert thinking: modeling of new concepts and skills – the 'how' of the lesson.
- Guided practice: practice facilitated by the teacher providing a gradual release.
- Closure: the final check for understanding before the teacher releases students to independent practice.
- Independent practice: practice new learning for fluency.

The order of delivery is approximate because the preview, learning objective, and review need to precede the presentation of key ideas in the lesson. The order of those three components is a professional decision by the teacher as to how best to present the new lesson to allow for the most coherent flow.

Tip #2. Don't shoot an OWL
You don't have to use a stopwatch but be aware of the time. Be done talking when students are done listening.[24]

MISCELLANEOUS ISSUES

Teach to the middle?
Some administrators or colleagues will tell teachers to teach to the middle level students. The rationale being that such a strategy will allow the middle and high students to understand the lesson. The lower level students who do not understand the lesson can be remediated at a later time. Other administrators and colleagues suggest teachers target the high performing students. The rationale being that such a strategy will benefit the high level students who are so often neglected.

Another rationale that is used for targeting the curriculum at higher performing students is to project high expectations for all students.

---

24   About one minute per year of age for OWL 1.

Theoretically the strategy will challenge and bring along some of the middle students. Once again, the low students will need to be remediated at another time so no need to worry about them – or so the rationale goes.

I disagree with structuring a lesson for a particular level of student. Lessons designed using the FAST Framework will identify the concepts and skills that need to be taught, and the level of rigor that must be learned by all students.[25]

Differentiate?

There has been much written about differentiating instruction for various student achievement levels and interests in a classroom. If the structure of the instruction matches how students learn (meaning that it is both effective and efficient) then differentiating instruction is not necessary. What will be differentiated are the students' work products.

The structure of a lesson does not change based on ability levels of the students in your class. The structure of lessons does not change based on reading levels, vocabulary levels, or other varying levels of any subskill. This framework works for *all* students. During training on the FAST Framework, it is not unusual to have teachers tell me, 'I just attended a GATE training and many of the ideas you are presenting are the same.' Or, at the same presentation, another teacher will approach and say, 'I just attended a special education training and they presented a lot of the same information for Universal Design.' Or teaching second language students, etc. A lesson structured to mirror how students learn will work for all students. What differs, based on ability levels, will be the specific strategies and examples that are used during the lesson. The structure does not change. The more expert a teacher becomes in understanding and applying the structure, the easier and quicker lesson planning becomes.

---

25 'Rigor' is another one of those words we use in education that everyone believes has a shared meaning, but in fact does not. Rigor, in this context, is used to mean the level of sophistication at which the students are expected to interact with the content. For example, while planning a lesson for a functional skills level class of special education students, the teacher chose the following learning objective, 'Students will properly plant seeds.' The concept for the students was to know that to properly plant seeds, the planting must be done in the order soil, seeds, and then more soil. It was the teacher's decision to teach this lesson at that level of rigor.

As you read through the following extended chapters on each component of the FAST Framework you will learn the science behind effective design and delivery. Cognitive load theory, briefly presented earlier in this chapter, was a foundational element upon which much of this framework was designed. You do not not need to become an expert on the research, but a basic reader's digest understanding of some pertinent elements of this theory will propel student learning as a result of more effective and efficient teaching.

NOTES FRO/\ THE FIELD

Most teachers with whom we work have never planned a coherent lesson. Many teachers have never been told that the learning objective must match the independent practice.

Most teachers with whom we work have never taken the time to fully develop the key ideas beyond thinking of the concepts as 'vocabulary'. Nor have many teachers taken the time to clearly understand the concepts themselves before they teach a lesson.

When teachers plan a lesson using the backwards planning procedure, they realize – some for the first time – the amount of specificity needed to minimize extraneous cognitive load.

After designing her first lesson using this procedure a teacher said to me, 'This is great! But we just spent an hour planning one lesson. I don't have an hour to plan every lesson.'

Another teacher with whom we previously worked happened to be walking by. I asked her how long it took her to plan a lesson using the FAST Framework. She replied, 'Maybe 10 to 15 minutes. Most time is spent finding and preparing materials. But I was doing that before.'

The most frequently viewed mistake in the design and delivery of lessons is attempting to teach too much content. Less is more.

The most effective way to plan a lesson that will address trying to teach too much is the backwards planning method prescribed in this chapter. Using the structure of the FAST Framework will facilitate planning decisions that will make lessons more manageable for all students.

Plan FAST. Teach FAST.

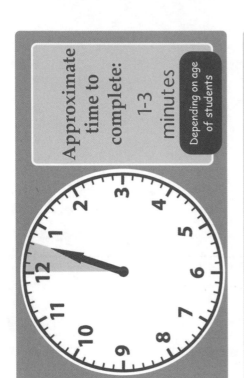

Approximate time to complete:
1-3 minutes

Depending on age of students

COMPONENT CONNECTIONS

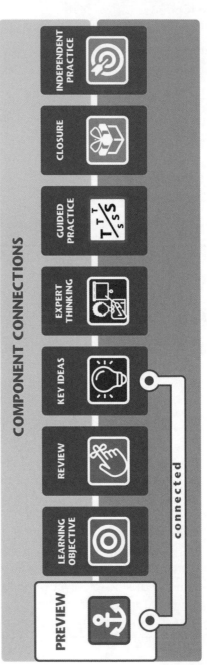

PREVIEW

LEARNING OBJECTIVE

REVIEW

KEY IDEAS

EXPERT THINKING

GUIDED PRACTICE

CLOSURE

INDEPENDENT PRACTICE

connected

CHAPTER 2
THE PREVIEW

Big ideas in the preview:

- Preview serves as a conceptual anchor.
- Prompts students' recall of relevant past experiences.
- Connects past experiences to new concepts in the lesson.
- These past experiences, or prior knowledge, are not necessarily a result of academic learning.
- Students are interested in lessons that relate to them personally.

OVERVIEW

We all learn new concepts by making connections to what we already know (aka prior knowledge). The purpose of the preview component is to help students connect prior knowledge to new concepts about to be presented in the lesson. An effective preview will help students to make connections using the students' existing schema. The prior knowledge unearthed from students' memories, will serve as an anchor upon which the new concepts are tethered.

This schematic anchor can be used by the teacher and students throughout the lesson. It provides the teacher with a class baseline of common experience to help students create new conceptual knowledge. These experiences allow the teacher to continuously compare and contrast or develop examples and non-examples. The conceptual anchor that is the preview allows all students to make conceptual connections as the new content will be just a small step within their zone of proximal development.[26]

The students' prior knowledge of the concepts does not have to be 'academic' or something that was previously learned in school. Their prior knowledge may be from a totally different context. It may be something that is known to the students simply because they have been alive and traveling through the world for their limited number of years.

The preview may also include a bit of intrigue, mystery, or discovery. For example, imagine a lesson with the following learning objective: interpret metaphors. The teacher begins the lesson by asking the students a question that includes the use of a metaphor, 'Students, if I said to you, "When my two-year-old daughter misses her nap she is a monster." What do you imagine my daughter is doing?'

The question demands that students reflect on what they already know about how people, including babies, act when they are tired. The question helps students connect their prior knowledge of the world (i.e. fussy, cranky babies) to the new content to be presented in the lesson (i.e. metaphors). Such connections make abstract concepts such as metaphors accessible to all students through concrete examples.

As stated in chapter 1, students have limited attention span.[27] It is imperative that the teacher assists students in making cognitively germane

---

26 The Zone of Proximal Development (ZPD) has been defined as: 'The distance between the actual developmental level as determined by independent problem solving and the level of potential development as determined through problem-solving under adult guidance, or in collaboration with more capable peers.' See Vygotsky, L. S. (1978) *Mind in society: The development of higher psychological processes.* Cambridge, MA, Harvard University Press, p. 86.

27 Students can attend to new information for approximately 5-20 minutes depending on their age and other factors.

connections as quickly as possible, usually within the first 1-2 minutes of the lesson.

RATIONALE FOR THE PREVIEW (AKA RESEARCH)

Our senses, and by extension, our brains are constantly being bombarded with stimuli. The mechanism in our brain that allows us to filter stimuli is called the reticular activating system. This reticular activating system operates like attention blinders on a stream of stimuli. Stated very crudely, it is continuously filtering stimuli and making decisions about which will be allowed to receive conscious attention and which will be blocked out.

Examples of this phenomenon are frequently experienced by everyone and so easily demonstrated. Have you ever been in a crowded room of people engaged in conversation when you hear your name spoken? Although you cannot identify the speaker, and they did not speak above the current level of conversation, you clearly hear your name. Among all the other possible stimuli that could gain your attention, one of the most well-known and familiar auditory utterances is perceived by you. The reticular activating system has made a decision to allow the utterance of your name to enter your consciousness and earn your attention.

Teachers must understand that even in a seemingly quiet, relatively non-visually stimulating environment, they are still competing with a plethora of other stimuli for their students' attention. This includes students' prior experiences as the students attempt to make sense of the world, e.g. the current lesson. In order to metaphorically move to the front of the attention line, teachers must introduce lessons in a manner that will draw and guide students from the familiar to the new. In new learning the mind moves from prior knowledge and connects it to similar conceptual knowledge. Through very intentional questioning, teachers can guide their students' attention to specific experiences and help them connect those experiences to the new learning.

All students need to connect prior learning, and prior experiences, to new concepts. Because *all* students need to make this connection the mechanics and strategies for engaging students with intentional questioning become critically important.

Many of the guidelines for engaging *all* students while checking for understanding (see appendix III) also apply to questioning in the preview.[28]

DESIGN TIPS

Tip #1. Questions are tied to the students' prior knowledge

The teacher should be 99.9% sure that students have had prior experiences related to those in the question being asked. These experiences do not have to be firsthand.

Tip #2. Questions about students' prior knowledge can relate to vicarious experiences

The students' experiences may belong to another person. For example, in the above example about the teacher's crying baby, the teacher may phrase a question/prompt like this, 'Raise your hand if you remember having a baby brother or sister in the house.' Or, 'Raise your hand if you have a friend who has a baby brother or sister in the house.' Or, 'Raise your hand if you have read a story, seen a movie or TV show about a baby in the house.' By making the prompts in this manner, vicarious knowledge is just as good as firsthand. The point is familiarity. And, if necessary, the teacher can provide experiences through short stories, short videos, etc.[29]

Tip #3. Avoid reading stories as a preview

A favorite introduction to lessons in primary grades is to read a story as an 'attention grabber'. There are several problems with reading stories to the class as the preview. First, if the story is entertaining then instead of focusing it becomes distracting. Second, the specific concept that should be the focus of the preview gets lost in other details in the story. Finally, it takes too long.

DELIVERY TIPS

Tip #1. Questions are directed to the entire class

Because it is important for all students to make the connection, questions should be directed to the entire class, not to individual students.

---

28   A teacher in South Carolina, a US Navy veteran, shared a mnemonic he had learned in the Navy for effective checking for understanding: APPLE. A – Ask a question, P – Pause, P – Pick a student(s), L – Listen, E – Elaborate or Explain.

29   Short, short, short! Remember all of this must happen within the first 1-3 minutes of the lesson.

Begin questions with, 'How many of you have ever _____?' Or, 'Have you, or someone you know ever _____?'

Tip #2. All students are given an opportunity to respond

All students must be given an opportunity to respond to someone, but not every student needs to share their response with the entire class. Hearing what a partner, or other students in a group share, may prompt more memories in students.

Tip #3. Provide constructive/instructive feedback to ensure students will make the proper connection

Earlier in the chapter, an example was given where a teacher told her students that her '... baby was a monster when she didn't get her nap.' Even though the connection – the baby is not really a monster – may seem obvious to the teacher, it may not be as obvious to the students. Because *all* students need to make the connection, the teacher should be *explicit* about how what the students already know is tied to the new lesson.

For example, in the above story about the teacher's 2-year-old who is a monster when missing her nap, the teacher must follow up student responses with an explicit connecting statement. 'Is my baby *really* a monster? Of course not. When I said she was a monster I meant she was so cranky and crying so loudly, that my baby was scary like a monster. She wasn't really a monster, but I compared how she behaved to how a monster behaves. When I used the word "monster" I didn't mean my baby was actually a monster. I was comparing my baby to a monster. Making a comparison like that is called a *metaphor*. Today we will be learning what metaphors are and how to figure out the meaning of metaphors.'[30]

Tip #4. Remember the time!

'How many of you have been to the beach?' asks the teacher. Every hand goes up. Every student wants to share. Don't let the excitement of the

---

30 Students at the grade level in which metaphors are introduced are familiar with various types of figurative language. They know a baseball player did not really hit the ball a mile. They know that when a teacher directs a student to hit the lights that the student does not need to make a fist. What the students are not familiar with are the various academic terms that name figurative language. The students know more than they think they know.

students over a question bleed into OWL 1. All students need to share with someone, but not everyone needs to share with the entire class.

It is the recall of the information that is important. Asking every child to share with the entire class is not necessary and can be counterproductive. You need to call on a few students in order to redirect attention to the critical elements (see above), but calling on many students simply takes too much time. Instead, when a student that is called on gives a response, simply ask the class, 'How many of you said something like that?' Plan on 1-3 minutes max.[31]

FREQUENTLY ASKED QUESTIONS

Q: What if students are not responding to the question?

A: You need to change your question. It can be scary.

This is what happened to me. Not long ago, a friend of mine allowed me to teach a writing lesson to her 4th grade students. The objective for the lesson was: 'Students will write position statements for a persuasive essay.'

All children are expert persuaders; sometimes also referred to by adults as manipulators. They have been persuading siblings, friends, and parents to fulfill desires for years. The students may not know the academic term 'persuasion', but they are certainly familiar with the concept. In order to connect the students' prior knowledge to the new academic concept I asked the class of 4th grade students the following question: 'How many of you have tried to convince your parents to let you spend the night at a friend's house?'

The response from the class was silence. I asked again, trying to prod an answer. My initial belief was the class was just being shy with a guest teacher. I waited patiently for someone to answer – for *anyone* to answer. At this point, even though I knew *all* students needed to be engaged with the question, in the midst of this uncomfortable situation, I would have wrongly settled for just one student. But, after about 15 more seconds, which seemed like an eternity, a student volunteered, 'I have never tried to convince my parents to let me spend the night at a friend's house, but

---

31   Often an effective preview can be done in about a minute.

I have tried to convince them to take me to McDonalds!' The entire class raised their hands excitedly. They, too, had tried to convince their parents to dine at McDonald's.

I exhaled a sigh of relief. My lesson was back on track.

'You all have tried to convince someone to do something,' I responded. 'Another word for convincing is persuading. Today we are going to learn how to persuade, or convince, someone to do something in writing.'

Be sure the question you ask to engage the students actually calls forth students' experiences.

Q: I was taught to ask a question like: 'Does anyone know what a metaphor is?' Is that a good preview question?

A: No, no, and no. It does not matter if a student thinks they know what a metaphor is. If they stick around for five minutes everyone will know what a metaphor is because that is what you will be teaching them. Students understand many concepts but may not know the academic term that names the concept. This type of question is just a time waster.

Q: Do you have any more examples from other disciplines?

A: Below are two examples of successful previews as reported by instructional coaches.

Special day class: Math
Recently one of my colleagues planned a math lesson with a special day class teacher.[32] As the teacher began to discuss the specific learning objective, focusing on converting exponents to expressions, she complimented the teacher (a first-year intern) on his judgement about limiting the scope of his learning objective to a learnable chunk of new information for his students. His response was, 'Well, I kind of have to do that or they end up in tears.'

Fast forward to the next day when the teacher began his lesson with the preview and drew 5 triangles on the board. 'When you were all in kindergarten, you used to play with blocks. If you lined up a row of

---

32 With thanks to my colleague Dr. Janae Tovar for both this anecdote and the following one regarding a science class about the periodic table.

triangles, and then lined up another row of triangles, what were you doing?' The students excitedly called out, 'Making a pattern!' He then asked, 'How many triangles are in this pattern?' Students chanted back to him, '5!' 'Well, today we're going to learn about exponents and expressions, which is pretty much what you already know about making patterns from kindergarten … but this is at middle school level.'

Smiles all around. Kids saying, 'Yes!' No tears. Open to learning about exponents!

Patterns became the anchor concept the teacher used to show that 5^2 was 5 x 5, just like 5^3 was 5 x 5 x 5, and just like 54 was 5 x 5 x 5 x 5. It is just a pattern.

High School: Science

The same colleague also worked with a young science teacher who was freshly out of the credential program. His first class was filled predominantly with freshmen and sophomores. He had assumed the job after the start of the school year and was still getting his footing with management of the students' behavior.

He was very enthusiastic about his new job and had a collection of fun ideas and activities to inspire the students. Still, he was uncertain about what he had in mind because of the tendency of his class to lose focus and become distracted.

They would be planning the initial lesson of a unit on the periodic table of elements. The objective was for the students to be able to navigate the chart, and then to understand what the various components represented by identifying specific information about any given element. For an introduction, the lesson was ambitious.

He started out their planning session by describing a 'preview' activity that would function like a mini-demonstration highlighting the attributes of two different elements. He envisioned himself behind the lab table at the front of the classroom performing the demonstration, while his students hovered around him to watch. He acknowledged that his students might get rowdy during the preview because they would be crowded together up front, or that they might waste time not getting up to the front of the room quickly enough. My colleague was in agreement with all the above.

Her question to him was, 'Does that have to be the preview?'

It sounded like a very engaging demonstration, but did it have to be the beginning of a lesson with so much other essential content? It did not specifically tie to the objectives of the lesson. It was certainly engaging, but the purpose of the activity was merely to excite the students about the content. 'Why couldn't the demonstration be at the end of the lesson or at another time in the unit?' she asked.

He taught the lesson using a preview that connected the table of elements to a road map. Just as a road map is structured, has symbols, and contains lots of information, so is the periodic table. It is also organized with symbols and an organizational structure that contains a lot of information about each element. He showed the kids how they could read the chart, and find all sorts of information about any element.

It was evident that he was still working on his classroom management, but the lesson went really well for a brand-new teacher on the job for only 5 weeks. The majority of students could navigate the table to locate an element, and identify its number of protons, electrons, and atomic mass. His students were successful and more on the task throughout the period because he had kept the preview focused and brief, allowing sufficient time and working memory for the new content.

An effective preview provides an anchor for both the teacher and students that both can return to throughout the lesson. If it is not an anchor from prior learning to the new content, then it is not a preview but a distraction from the key ideas, competing for working memory.

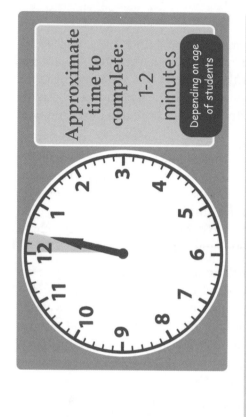

Approximate
time to
complete:
1-2
minutes

Depending on age
of students

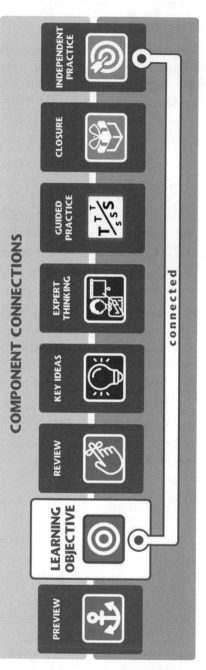

COMPONENT CONNECTIONS

PREVIEW

LEARNING
OBJECTIVE

REVIEW

KEY IDEAS

EXPERT
THINKING

GUIDED
PRACTICE

$\frac{T^T{}^T}{S^S}$

CLOSURE

INDEPENDENT
PRACTICE

connected

CHAPTER 3
LEARNING OBJECTIVES

Big ideas in learning objectives:

- Learning objectives match independent practice exactly.
- Provide clarity and focus to the entire lesson.
- Teach one objective at a time.
- Should be written simply.

OVERVIEW

Any discussion of learning objectives is sure to bring eye rolls from a large majority of teachers. I am sure that there is not a teacher anywhere who has not been lectured about the importance of learning objectives. I am sure that there is not a teacher anywhere who has not been told that learning objectives should be posted prominently in the classroom. I agree. Clear learning objectives are important for students and teachers.

There are proclamations and opinions about learning objectives made by others that differ from mine. One important difference of opinion is how complicated the writing of a learning objective needs to be. A quick internet search about how to write learning objectives will yield articles that claim there are three parts of a well written learning objective. There is also no shortage of articles that explain and argue for four important parts of an objective. After reading about the five important parts of the learning objective I decided to call it quits.

It may not be established science whether a learning objective should have three, four, five, or more parts. But, it is clear that a specific and clear learning objective provides guidance to both students and teachers. A clear objective informs students what is expected of them during a learning episode. Equally important, a clear objective provides teachers with a roadmap to choose appropriate materials, activities, and formative assessments.

LEARNING OBJECTIVE EXACTLY MATCHES INDEPENDENT PRACTICE

At the end of the last century schools faced harsh criticism regarding the underperformance of many students. One of the solutions instituted by the Federal Government was to sanction schools whose test scores did not meet a targeted standard. This brought outrage from many schools and educators.

One of the main criticisms of these sanctions was that it created a testing culture versus a learning culture. The critics argued that the assessments being given to students did not measure what was being taught. The criticism was valid. It made sense that students should only be tested on content they had been taught; or were supposed to have been taught.

The assessments that most schools were directed to use at the time were norm-referenced tests that are used to provide students with percentile rankings that compare their performance to other students. Educators argued that these assessments should be changed to criterion referenced tests.[33] Criterion-referenced tests assess students' knowledge of grade-level standards.

---

33   Norm-referenced assessments may have test items that ask students about content that was not part of the grade-level curriculum. The purpose of the assessment is to provide a means to compare students' performances. Criterion referenced assessments measure performance against what students should have learned based on grade-level standards.

The data gleaned from a criterion-based assessment could be used to evaluate not only individual students, but entire classrooms, entire grade-levels, and the completeness of the taught curriculum. The norm-referenced assessments provided no such data.

The criterion-referenced assessments, and the data they provided, became useful. Now the assessments aligned with the curriculum. If the student had been successful learning the curriculum then that success should be reflected in the assessment. The alignment of the curriculum with assessments is fundamental.

Just as the curriculum is the learning goal for the year, the learning objective is the learning goal for the lesson. Just as the curriculum has an assessment that aligns, the learning objective has an assessment that aligns. The assessment for the lesson is independent practice. The learning objective should not only *align* with the independent practice, but it should *match it exactly*.

The success of a lesson should only be judged one way: at the conclusion of the lesson were the students able to successfully complete the independent practice that exactly matched the learning objective?[34]

If the success of the lesson is judged by students ability to complete the independent practice, it is only fair that this practice matches the lesson.

Textbooks do not always follow this dictum. It is not uncommon for a textbook, and Teacher's Edition of that text, to provide a lesson for a teacher to follow, then provide independent practice that does not match what was taught. Teachers become frustrated because although they executed the prescribed lesson plan, students are not able to successfully complete the independent practice. Students become frustrated because although they thought they were understanding and following the lesson it was different from the assigned independent practice.

---

34   There is always a question as to what percentage of students need to be successful. Some say teachers should shoot for 80%. Some say 90%. Some elementary teachers do not use percentages. Some teachers have the goal of all students minus the number of students who can sit around the kidney shaped table in the back of the room (the table used for group instruction). The answer will vary from lesson to lesson but will be between 4-6 students, who will get immediate in-class intervention.

Like criterion-referenced assessments that provide useful data on students' performance at the end of the school year, independent practice should provide daily data on students' performance at the end of a lesson.

CLARITY AND FOCUS FOR THE LESSON

Various issues are discussed in the plethora of articles written about learning objectives. But what *all* these articles have in common is that the learning objective should promote clarity for both students and teachers through clear actionable verbs such as 'identify', 'classify', 'explain', 'solve' – as opposed to less specific verbs such as 'know', 'understand', 'discuss' or 'think about'. For example, a learning objective that states, 'Students will identify extended metaphors in a poem,' provides much more clarity than the objective, 'Students will understand how authors use extended metaphors in poems.' The latter objective begs the question, 'What does it mean to "understand"?'

Well written learning objectives provide clarity by providing limitations on what will be included in the lesson. Limitations, or constraints, are helpful to both the students and the teacher.[35] The universe of knowledge can seem overwhelming. Constraints and limits inform both the teacher and the students what the lesson is not about.

Learning objectives are constrained and limited by specific predictable language. A learning objective is a simply stated sentence that tells students what concept they will be learning and what skill will be used to demonstrate that concept. Learning objectives contain a noun, that will identify the concept addressed in the lesson, and a verb that will identify the skill used to engage with the concept.[36] In the example above: 'Students will identify extended metaphors in a poem,' *extended metaphors* is the noun that identifies the concept, and *identification* is the skill that will be taught to the students to engage with extended metaphors.

---

35 This phrase, ' ... helpful to both teachers and students,' is repeated over and over again. That learning objectives are beneficial to both teachers and students is another argument for their importance.

36 Learning objectives may contain more than one noun, but there is always a noun that identifies the central concept, or key idea, of the lesson.

Examples of learning objectives:

Students will analyze rhetorical devices in a political speech.

Students will estimate the square root of a non-perfect square.

Students will analyze third party presidential candidates.

Students will punctuate complex sentences.

Students will add two-digit numbers using regrouping.

Students will analyze metaphors.

Students will explain two events that led to the abolition of slavery.

Students will subtract a one-digit number from a two-digit number using regrouping.

DECIDING ON A LEARNING OBJECTIVE: CHUNKING FOR INSTRUCTION

There are also many articles for educators that discuss the importance of chunking or limiting the amount of information presented in lessons to mitigate issues of extraneous cognitive load and working memory.[37] Learning objectives clarify the amount of content to be delivered in a single learning episode. Learning objectives identify the chunks.

Literature regarding chunking and sequencing addresses two learning concerns. The first, as described above, is to limit the amount of information in any one lesson. The second, is that proper chunking and sequencing can aid in the design of focused and deliberate practice, leading to the memorization of concepts and skills.

There are many valid strategies to chunk information for memorization. However, in this chapter we are more concerned with chunking, and sequencing concepts and skills, for the purposes of learning and understanding. This means creating a stair step of lessons that lead to more and more complex applications.

---

37   See chapter 1.

There are a number of cliches that describe the impact of breaking tasks down into smaller chunks.[38]

- 'The man who removes a mountain begins by carrying away small stones', Chinese proverb.
- 'The journey of a thousand miles begins with one step', Lao Tzu.
- 'For the great doesn't happen through impulse alone, and is a succession of little things that are brought together', Vincent Van Gogh.
- 'It's the little details that are vital. Little things make big things happen', John Wooden.

Sayings become cliches because they are true. The wisdom of breaking large tasks into smaller more manageable chunks goes back literally thousands of years. Breaking large tasks, i.e. the standards, into teachable chunks for students is a critical part of the teacher's job.

A major goal of education is to help students understand and apply content, not simply remember information. Therefore, when we discuss chunking, we mean the breaking down of information into chunks that are conceptually rich, intact, *and* that do not over-tax the working memory.[39]

The perils of teachers trying to teach too much in a particular lesson cannot be overstated. Attempting to teach too much during a particular learning episode is the most frequently observed reason for lessons not being as successful as they could be. Limiting the amount of content can help students remember information. Oft repeated suggestions for chunking are:

- Break large amounts of information into smaller amounts.
- Identify similarities or patterns.
- Organize the information.
- Group information into manageable units.

---

38   You can search Google to find dozens of such admonitions.

39   Intact in this sense means *to avoid deconstructing* to such an extent that although students are successful, they only accomplish something that lacks stand alone meaning outside of the context of the class.

All of these suggestions are good advice and reflect strategies that address concerns presented in the original research by George Miller on the limitations of working memory.

TEACH ONE OBJECTIVE AT A TIME

Learning objectives are teachable chunks of information that are designed to be learned in a single learning episode. Only one new learning objective is taught during a learning episode. From a teacher's perspective there are several arguments for doing this. Teaching only one chunk mitigates the problem of teaching too much. Also a single objective helps the teacher identify and analyze the pertinent formative data collected during the lesson. Teaching more than one objective during a lesson confounds student data. It becomes impossible for the teacher to diagnose a student's problem if multiple objectives are being taught. Which of the multiple objectives is causing problems for the student? What is the proper mediation strategy?

From the perspective of the student, limiting lessons to a single objective allows students to focus on one thing at a time. This focus allows students to become more reflective learners, or in the vernacular, the students become meta-learners.

There have been teachers and administrators who have pushed back on the notion of limiting a lesson to a single learning objective. They argue that students need to use skills and knowledge from prior lessons as they move forward with the new content. Of course they do! I absolutely agree. Embedding content from prior lessons, as well as constituent skills and knowledge, is critical to giving students practice and repetition. But the important distinction is that the new learning is the identified learning objective.

The new learning is the focus of the lesson. Prior learning is not neglected. Prior learning is embedded into practice supporting the new objective. However, the formative data, and resulting teacher actions, are based on the new learning: the single learning objective in the new lesson. Lessons with a single learning objective are more efficient, i.e. faster.

DESIGN TIPS

Tip #1. Keep it short and simple (unlike this explanation)

Earlier in this chapter it was stated that there is debate in academic circles regarding what should be included in a well written learning objective. Those academics who argue for four or five elements say that a well written learning objective should include what students will be doing during the lesson such as, 'Students, while working with a partner will discuss ...' Other academics even say that a well written learning objective should include how students will demonstrate their knowledge of the lesson by including language such as , 'Students will demonstrate their knowledge of the content by answering five questions at the end of the lesson.' Yet other academics argue that a well written learning objective tells the students what they are going to do by including the phrase, 'Students will be able to ...' (this has been abbreviated on whiteboards across the country as SWBAT). Including phrases such as these do not contribute to students' understanding.

Earlier in this chapter a sample learning objective was provided for a lesson on extended metaphors. Below are two examples of that learning objective. Example #1 is written in the manner recommended by many authorities described above. Example #2 is the shortened, simplified version.

Example #1.

At the end of the lesson, SWBAT identify the extended metaphors in the poem 'Oh Captain! My Captain!' by Walt Whitman. Students will meet in groups to discuss the poem before writing a paragraph identifying the metaphors used by the author.

Example #2.

Students will identify extended metaphors in literature.

The additional verbiage in Example #1 may serve to inform the teacher, but it does not add value for the students. In the best case this language is distracting for students. In the worst case the extraneous information is overwhelming. Students quickly discover that they do not need to know all of the information in the learning objective at this point in the lesson, so they learn to ignore it. Remember that you have a limited amount of time in OWL 1 to teach key ideas and explain expert thinking; you do not have the luxury of time to spend on an overlong learning objective.

Still not convinced? Let's address the problems with each one of the suggestions above separately.

- *Including how the students will behave, or what strategies will be employed by the teacher.* The teacher absolutely must plan what the students will do during the lesson. However, telling students that they will get in groups and be given different tasks (or whatever will happen) does not need to be included in the learning objective, because students will need to be directed later in the lesson anyway. Tasks are not clear to students when they have no idea what will be taught in the lesson; they have no context. The time to tell students what they are going to do is right before they are going to do it. Giving them too much information too early is confusing and contributes to extraneous cognitive load.

- *Including how students will demonstrate knowledge.* This is very similar to above. Trying to explain to students what they are going to be doing before they have any idea about the lesson is distracting. And, more importantly, the learning objective always matches the independent practice exactly.

- *'Students Will Be Able To...' (SWBAT).* Again as above, it is distracting to students when this information is presented at the beginning of the lesson. It does not add anything. Who do we think will be doing the work?

Just in case the horse we are flogging is not dead enough, here is an anecdote about writing learning objectives. Several years ago, at the height of school and district sanctions, I was training teachers in the FAST Framework. After explaining the importance of learning objectives, and the importance of writing them in a manner that students could understand, I was informed by several teachers that the school district required teachers to write learning objectives in a very prescriptive manner (which of course was absolutely contrary to what I had told them.) Below is an example of the manner that teachers were expected to write learning objectives:

SWBAT [students will be able to] identify and interpret extended metaphors in the poem, 'O' Captain! My Captain!' By Walt Whitman. Students will use a graphic organizer provided by the teacher to identify at least three metaphors and provide a paragraph interpreting those three metaphors.

As stated in this chapter, during our training we teach that learning objectives do not need to be so expansive. We would write the above objective in a more simple manner:

Students will identify and interpret extended metaphors in poems.

A learning objective stated in this manner is sufficient because by definition learning objectives should match independent practice exactly. The second sentence is superfluous because it is merely a description of the independent practice.

While my words were still hanging in the air several teachers raised their hands. 'We have been told that the learning objective must include how the students will meet the objective.' The teachers in the training were directing their gaze between me and the administrators who were also in the training.[40] I am experienced enough to know that I should not get in the middle of the teachers and what their administration has to say. The assistant superintendent for curriculum and instruction, who was in the training, told the group that the administrators and I would meet at lunch to discuss the issue.

During lunch the administration reiterated the sanctions the district was operating under. This included teams of educators briefly observing classrooms. The administrators stated that the more descriptive objectives allowed the observers to be very clear on what was being taught during walkthroughs.[41] They argued that the completeness of the learning objective format that they were requiring provided all the information needed by the observers.

As a way to satisfy the administrators' needs, I suggested the teachers make available a copy of the independent practice associated with the lesson. Using this strategy, the learning objectives would be more concise and

40 This is a perfect example of why we do not do teacher training without administrators present in the room. I have been in enough rodeos to avoid being roped into issues that are beyond the scope of my authority.

41 In other words, the learning objective was being written for the observers not the students or the teacher.

student friendly, and the administrators would have even more complete information regarding expected student outcomes for the lesson.

After lunch the teachers were informed, they would no longer be required to write the long, complicated, and cumbersome learning objectives. Instead, a spot in the room would be designated where independent practice would be placed so that observers could review what students would be expected to do. The administration realized that what was being asked of the teachers had become unduly burdensome. The needs of students, teachers, and administrators could be met in an alternative manner that made the instruction even better.

Whatever is asked of teachers must make sense. Focused instruction is quality instruction. Quality will always subsume compliance.

Writing learning objectives that are concise, that clearly define the concept and skill to be learned and demonstrated in the lesson, will always be sufficient if the FAST Framework is followed.

Tip #2. Use academic language

There is another prescription for learning objectives that is often given. It is the admonition that learning objectives be written in 'kid friendly' language, i.e. no academic language allowed. The argument for kid friendly language is that learning objectives that contain specialized language from the discipline will not be understood by students. In addition to not being understood, they could also be intimidating. For example, they would argue that students reading the learning objective, 'Students will analyze the use of rhetorical devices in political speeches,' will become confused and intimidated because they do not know what 'rhetorical devices' are. Or, they might not know what 'political speeches' are.

My response: of course, the students do not know what rhetorical devices are. That is why the lesson is being taught! By the end of the lesson, students will not only know what rhetorical devices are, they will be analyzing the use of such devices in speeches.[42]

---

42 If an effective preview occurs prior to the reading of the learning objective (see previous chapter) students will realize that they do in fact know what 'rhetoric' is, they just don't know the academic name for it.

Do not sell students short. Do not sell yourself short. Use the language of the standards. Use the language of the discipline. If the standards use academic language and/or language from the discipline, use that language. Train your students that it is okay not to know something at the beginning of the lesson. That is why they are in school.

Tip #3. Describe the independent practice

There are might be times when you are having a difficult time expressing the learning objective. Remember, the learning objective and independent practice match exactly. If you know what you want the students to do at the end of the lesson then just describe the independent practice and abracadabra! You have your learning objective.

DELIVERY TIPS

Tip #1. Display the learning objective

The learning objective should be written and displayed in the classroom where it will be visible the entire lesson. This is true even for emergent readers. Learning objectives will contain high frequency words that will assist in remembering not only the learning objective but also provide practice reading the high frequency words.

Tip #2. Read the learning objective to the students

Read the learning objective to the students. Then ask students to chorally read the objective with you. Take note of any words in the objective that may be unfamiliar or difficult to pronounce. Practice saying those words with the students. For example, the Teacher says: 'Students will describe objects using adjectives. Students let's say the word "adjectives" together. Ready? Adjectives. One more time. Adjectives.'

Students in all grades should chorally read the learning objective at least once after the teacher has read the objective. Yes, students in upper grades can read the objective.

Having the students read the learning objective once or twice is plenty. We have witnessed teachers directing the students to read the learning objective as many as seven or eight times. Do not beat a dead horse.

'Let's read the objective together.'

'Let's do that one more time.'

'Now, just this side of the room.'

'Now just that side.'

'Now just the boys.'

'Now just the girls.'

This is just a waste of time. Students have not gained any understanding of the lesson reading words out of context. Get on with the lesson. Tick tock, tick tock. [43]

---

43   Remember, you have a limited amount of time during OWL 1.

Approximate
time to
complete:
2-5
minutes

Depending on age
of students

COMPONENT CONNECTIONS

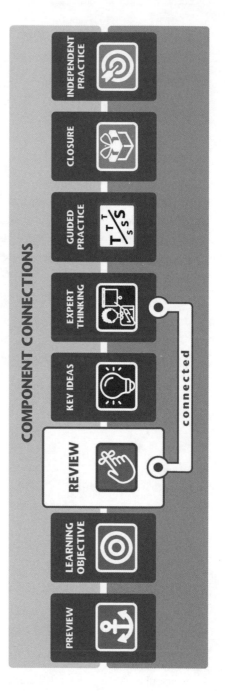

PREVIEW

LEARNING
OBJECTIVE

REVIEW

KEY IDEAS

EXPERT
THINKING

GUIDED
PRACTICE

CLOSURE

INDEPENDENT
PRACTICE

connected

CHAPTER 4
REVIEW

Big ideas in review:

- Review connects prior knowledge to new skills.
- Prior knowledge is a result of academic experiences.
- Students perform the review by answering teacher queries.
- Content and context of review is determined by new skill in lesson.

OVERVIEW

When training teachers in the FAST Framework, I often ask the group if any of their students have learning gaps. The teachers' response is always laughter. Of course, their students have learning gaps!

What is most interesting about the teachers' responses is not that their students have learning gaps, but that it does not matter if they work in a struggling school, or a high achieving school. The response is always the same. There will always be students who have some type of gap in their knowledge that must be bridged if those students are to make progress to meet grade-level expectations.

Because of the sequential nature of curricula, understanding the review component of the FAST Framework is very important. The review serves two purposes. First, the review facilitates students' retrieval of critical constituent skills from long-term memory to working memory.[44] In other words, even though students may have learned skills in a previous lesson, they may not be able to easily retrieve the skills from long-term memory without specific prompting. The teacher's prompts help students connect prior skills to the new skills in the lesson. Secondly, the review helps the teacher identify what scaffolding needs to be provided, and for which students.[45]

REVIEW VS PREVIEW

Although both review and preview connect students' prior knowledge to new learning, there is a major distinction between the two. The preview connects students' prior *conceptual knowledge* to new concepts in the lesson. The review connects students' prior *constituent skills* to new skills in the lesson.

In the preview, the prior conceptual knowledge may have been learned as a result of just being alive and existing in the world. For example, prior to a lesson on characterization, a teacher may ask students to describe something their best friends said or did that demonstrates why they are a good friend. Even a six-year-old can provide an answer. Students may respond by saying their best friend says nice things, is generous with toys,

---

44 Usually the term 'subskills' is employed to describe the necessary set of skills one must possess in addition to the new skills learned in lesson. The prefix 'sub' implies that these skills are not as important, or in some way subordinate, to the new skills in the lesson. However, these skills are critical to new learning and are not subordinate in any way. On this basis I prefer the term 'constituent skills', which I have borrowed from Merriënboer and Kirschner (2013). See Merriënboer, J. and Kirschner, P. (2013) *Ten Steps to Complex Learning: A systematic approach to four component instructional design.* 2nd Ed. Routledge, NY.

45 Scaffolding is another one of those words we use in education and assume there is a shared meaning. I use the term 'scaffolding' to describe a work-around for when a student is not fluent in a constituent skill, in order to decrease cognitive load in the new lesson.

always shares lunch, etc. Conceptually, the student understands that we can know someone is 'nice' by what they do, what they say, what they think, and what others say about them.

That knowledge (conceptual knowledge) – why we like someone – does not need to be taught by the classroom teacher. What needs to be taught by the teacher is how authors let readers know about characters. Authors develop characters by providing readers with information about what characters do, what they say, what they think, and what others say about them. In a preview teachers can thus tie the students' prior knowledge of friends to the literary concept of characterization.

In the review, teachers also prompt students to recall prior learning and make connections to the new learning. The review differs in two major aspects. First, whereas the purpose of the preview is to connect concepts learned in the past to new conceptual learning, the purpose of the review is to connect *skills* learned in the past to the new skills in the lesson. Second, in contrast to the preview where the prior concept *may not* have been learned as a result of classroom experience, the skills that are being reviewed *were previously taught in school.*

Teachers frequently ask, 'If the skill was supposed to have been learned in the prior grade, or in a prerequisite course, is it necessary to review it?' With all due respect to all previous teachers, if you did not personally teach the material just assume the students do not remember. Treat the content as new material and devote an entire lesson teaching it. If the students remember the content while you are teaching it the lesson should go quickly.

WHICH GAPS IN STUDENT KNOWLEDGE DO YOU ADDRESS FOR TODAY'S LESSON?

Sometimes individual students, or even entire classes, have major gaps in the constituent skills necessary for the new lesson. As noted in chapter 1, there is a limited amount of time to complete the preview, learning objective, and review without encroaching on OWL 1 (Optimal Window of Learning).[46] Given this limited amount of time, how does a teacher

---

46   Plan to spend no longer than 3-5 minutes on the review.

decide which skills to review? And, how does a teacher complete the review in such a limited amount of time?

Because students have learning gaps, and there is limited time to review, teachers must have a strategy for determining what to review. Although the review component occurs early in the delivery of the lesson, determining 'what' to review occurs late in the planning process. No decision about what needs to be reviewed should be made before the teacher has decided on the steps in the procedure. By waiting until the steps in the procedure have been determined, teachers can look to the steps to make decisions about which constituent skills will be needed in the new lesson.

The steps inform the teacher of exactly which specific concepts and skills the students need to know. If the skills in the steps are part of the new lesson, then the students will learn those skills in the new lesson. If the concepts or skills have been previously taught, then those concepts and skills will be part of the review. For example, to teach a lesson with the following learning objective: Subtract a one-digit number from a two-digit number using regrouping.

Sample problem:
$$\begin{array}{r} 13 \\ -\ 6 \\ \hline \end{array}$$

The procedure (or expert thinking) the teacher might present to the class would be as follows:

Step 1: Analyze – sufficient number of ones to subtract?

Step 2: Regroup if necessary.

Step 3: Subtract.

Step 4: Is answer reasonable?

The teacher should look at each step and ask herself, 'Will I teach this as part of the new lesson? Or, do I need to review this?'[47] By analyzing the steps in this manner the teacher can make a reasoned decision on what needs to be reviewed. There are many skills students lack. You cannot remediate them all in 3-5 minutes.

---

47 Teaching, in this context, includes checking for understanding to assertain who does not know the information.

It is only by analyzing the procedure in this manner that a teacher can ensure that everything students need to be successful in the new lesson has been taught, reviewed, or scaffolded.

WHAT IS THE BIG DEAL ABOUT THE REVIEW?

The principal purpose of the review is to facilitate students' retrieval of previously learned skills and concepts from long-term memory. Retrieval only occurs when a student is asked to answer some type of question.

The common use of the term 'review' implies that the teacher will be reviewing by providing another iteration of necessary identified constituent skills that have previously been taught; at least once. But an effective review is not the teacher telling. An effective review is the teacher asking. If all a teacher needed to do was to 'tell' students just one more time, what a wonderful world it would be!

Cognitive scientists tell us the most effective way to study, to recall information, to learn information, is to be 'tested' on that information.[48] The research describes testing in a very broad manner. Testing can be quizzes, exams, or in the case of an effective review, the asking of pertinent questions, i.e. questions that require recall of previously taught knowledge and skills.

There is not a teacher alive who would say they do not currently review information with their students. The question, of course, is the review effective? Below are two common examples of ineffective reviews which I have observed.[49]

Math example (what not to do)

Math curricula are very linear. For students to be successful today, the student needed to be successful yesterday. How do you ensure students were successful doing yesterday's lesson? The answer that most math teachers choose is to 'go over' yesterday's homework as a review.[50]

---

48 Agarwal, P. K. & Bain, P. M. (2019) *Powerful Teaching: Unleash the Science of Learning.* San Francisco, CA: Jossey-Bates.

49 Ineffective instructional practices are by definition time wasters. Tick tock, tick tock.

50 The reason 'go over' is in quotes is because it is such a nebulous term. Going over can mean, depending on the teacher, correcting, showing corrected answers, checking off that it has been done, doing what has been described in the paragraph below, or any combination of the above.

The most commoly observed method for 'going over' homework is to ask students if they have any questions about any problems from the homework assignment that the students would like the teacher to review.[51]

As the students call out the problems they would like to have the teacher 'review', the teacher notes the number of the problems on the board. Then the teacher dutifully proceeds to solve each of the problems while the class observes. This type of review is as common as it is problematic.

It is problematic for several reasons. First, usually the students who raise their hands to ask about a homework problem that they had difficulty solving are the top students in the class. These are also frequently the most motivated students and the ones who typically care most about getting the correct solution to a particular problem.

Second, the rest of class does not actually observe. Usually, the only student paying attention to the teacher's solution of any particular problem is the student who selected the problem in the first place. The rest of the students will have checked out for now. They are either waiting for their problem to be solved, waiting for the new lesson, or waiting for the end of the period.

The final reason it is ineffective – and surely the most frustrating to the teacher – is that when the teacher is nearly done solving the problem, 83% of the time the student who asked for the problem to be solved will declare, 'Never mind. I just made an addition mistake' (or whatever … a careless mistake that did not inhibit their understanding).[52]

Instead of having students determine which problems will be re-examined during the review, the teacher should select homework problems containing the constituent skills that are most critical for the new lesson.[53] Those select few problems are then assigned to students prior to the new lesson.

---

51 Can you see the problem already? What percentage of the class does not do homework? What percentage of the struggling students do homework?

52 I made the percentage up but whatever the true figure is it must be very high. In one high school I observed the average amount of time spent 'going over' homework was 19 minutes. That 'whoosh' sound you heard just now was the first OWL flying by.

53 The teacher knows which problems to select because she has already designed the procedure for the new lesson (see chapter 3).

In the worst case, the teacher will need to quickly solve the review problems she selected (after the students have already solved or attempted to solve them). At this time she can emphasize the constituent skills needed. Students should then be given an opportunity to 'compare and repair' their answers.

English language arts example (what not to do)

I was scheduled to observe a high school English teacher's literature lesson. When I arrived for the observation the teacher informed me he would be using the first ten minutes of the class to review figurative language terms. 'I have been reviewing these terms for a month and they still don't know them,' he told me.

For the first ten minutes of class the teacher referred to a list of figurative language terms on the screen in the front of the class. He read each term. He gave a definition of each term. He gave examples of each term. When he was done he began the literature lesson. When we had a chance to chat, he said, 'I have been doing that review for a month and they still don't know those terms!' An effective review is the teacher asking. An ineffective review is the teacher telling.[54]

DESIGN TIPS

Tip #1. Decide on the review after designing the procedure

See above, 'Which gaps in students knowledge do you address for today's lesson?'

Tip #2. Review questions should match to the new lesson in both content and context

The following anecdote about another ineffective review demonstrates the importance of this tip.[55] While I was observing a middle school language

---

54   This review gets double negative points. Knowledge of figurative language was not even necessary for the new lesson. The teacher not only wasted 10 minutes doing an ineffective review, but he also wasted 10 minutes that could have been used by students to practice the new content.

55   The reason for including so many 'how not to do a review' anecdotes in this chapter is because these examples could be raised to archetype status. Please do not do these. Teaching is hard enough already.

arts class that contained a high percentage of EL students, the teacher directed the students to the learning objective that was written on the board:

Learning objective: students will determine the appropriate definition of multiple meaning words by using the dictionary.

The rationale for the lesson was that most multiple meaning words function as either a noun or a verb. In order for a student to look up a multiple meaning word in a dictionary, online or using a hard copy, they must first identify if it was being used as a noun or a verb.

The teacher, after looking at the procedure she had designed for this learning objective, realized that students needed to be able to determine if an identified multiple meaning word was serving as a noun or a verb.[56] So, the teacher determined she would review nouns and verbs.

The teacher asked her 8th grade class, 'What is a noun?'

Not a single student responded. The teacher waited, and then repeated the question, 'Come on guys, what is a noun? I know you know this. What is a noun?'

The teacher was absolutely correct. EL or not, 8th grade students know what a noun is. After several more attempts to cajole an answer, she finally exasperatedly said, 'A noun: a person, place, thing or idea! Come on! You know that!'

She continued, 'Okay, someone give me an example of a noun.'

The teacher experienced the same lack of response to this question as there was to the first question. She repeated it. Then she said, 'Come on guys! Give me an example of a noun.'

She rattled a small can that was filled with popsicle sticks that contained the students' names. 'I am going to pull a stick,' she threatened.

No response.[57] No response.[58] Flustered, she pounded a student desk, 'A desk! A desk!' Then picking up a book, 'A book! A book! Come on you guys. You know this!'

---

56   'High five!'

57   'Bueller?'

58   'Bueller?'

What did she do next? She asked the class, 'What's a verb?'

The class responded, or rather did not respond, as they had to the previous questions.

The main problem with this review was there was a mismatch between the skills needed to perform the review and the skills that will be needed to be successful in the new lesson.

Not once during the lesson would the students have to give the definition of a noun or a verb. What the students *did* have to do was identify an underlined word in a sentence and determine if it was a noun or a verb. Such as: 'The <u>bark</u> is on the tree.'

If the teacher had given the students a sentence such as the one above, the students could then be directed to write on their whiteboards either V for verb or N for noun. That would practice the skill the students were being asked to use in the lesson. In this way the students would have had the opportunity to recall the information about nouns and verbs in the same context as they would be asked in the lesson. By reviewing content in the same context as needed for the new lesson, the resulting data can be used by the teacher to guide the lesson.

The teacher correctly chose what to review. But she missed the mark on how to review. Her review did not match in either content or context. It ended up being a waste of time. Tick tock, tick tock.

Tip #3. Teacher chooses the problems to review

The teacher should choose 2-3 problems from the previous day's independent practice or homework that contain the constituent skills needed for the new lesson.[59] Those problems should then be written on the board. The teacher directs all the students to solve the problems. The result of performing the review in this manner is that students will have had 2-3 more repetitions to solve problems with the identified constituent skills necessary for the new lesson.

Next, because the new procedure includes the constituent skills, students will have the opportunity to observe the teacher perform two more

---

59 The problems may come directly from independent practice or homework. Or, the problems may be new but very similar to those activities.

repetitions of the prerequisite skills during expert thinking, modeling. Now we are up to an additional 4-5 repetitions, in context. During guided practice, the students will use the constituent skills doing at least three more problems. Now we are up to 8 repetitions. An effective closure will add another.

If the students still need additional help, an immediate intervention after the lesson is appropriate.

By having all students solve the selected problems the teacher is also able to collect data about the proficiency level of the class. If everyone is good then the teacher can move on. If there is one particular issue that is prevalent in the data, then the teacher can provide some additional instruction to remediate the issue. In addition to providing additional instruction, the teacher can design scaffolding for those students who need it during the new lesson.[60]

Tip #4. A review problem can also serve as a preview
Many times math lessons will focus on several skills around a single concept for multiple days. The subtraction lesson earlier in this chapter is an example of just that. The concept identified in that lesson was place value. By having the students solve a subtraction problem that had embedded the concept of place value, a single problem addresses both review (by practicing the necessary constituent skill), and the preview (by having students recall prior conceptual learning).

DELIVERY TIPS

Tip #1. Do not give any hints or tips on how to perform the review problems
By not providing any hints, cues, or tips on how to answer review questions, the teacher will get more reliable data on what the students remember or do not remember.

After the students have had an opportunity to perform a previously learned skill, and they have been successful, you are ready to proceed with the new lesson. If students have been less than successful, provide feedback and a brief reminder that may be helpful.

---

60   See chapter 9.

Remember you only have a few minutes for the entire review. You cannot remediate anyone in that amount of time.

Tip #1a. Prior to students answering the review questions, provide a one minute refresher on the review questions

I know, I know. This is exactly opposite of Tip #1. Some teachers like to do the review cold like in Tip #1.[61] Others like to do a quick reminder first.

Tip #2. Give feedback to the entire class

The review is a time to collect data. Give specific feedback to the entire class. Individual students will know if the feedback applies to them. Remember you only have a few minutes. You cannot remediate anyone in that amount of time.[62]

Tip #3. Leave the review on the board

The constituent skill(s) represented in the review will come up again during the new lesson. Students who need additional reminding can use the worked example. Also, when you get to a particular step in the new procedure, you can say, 'This step is just like the review problem on the board'.

FREQUENTLY ASKED QUESTIONS

Q: What if all students are unable to perform the constituent skills?

A: It is very, very rare that even after the review all students will not be able to perform the identified constituent skills necessary for the new lesson. But, if all students cannot perform the constituent skills, in the context in which they will be asked in the new lesson, then you need to teach a lesson on those skills.

---

61   I am one who likes to do the review cold. Maybe it is because I am lazy. I figure if the students are successful, I don't need to take a minute to provide feedback. If they are not successful, I am not out anything.

62   If you think you just read that you are correct. It bears repeating. It is difficult for teachers not to help students immediately when they aren't able to perform a task.

Q: Are you saying I shouldn't go over homework?

A: No. I am saying the teacher should control what is reviewed. Teachers should select which homework problems need to be reviewed based on what is needed for the new lessons.[63]

Teachers have shared several different ways in which they 'go over' homework. Some teachers project correct answers on the board for students who are interested. This is best done after closure of the new lesson.

Q: What if the review will take more than 5 minutes?

A: If you believe the review will need to be extensive, meaning it will take more than the 3-5 minutes available, then you need to make a decision about how to best effectively review constituent skills.

One way to do an effective extended review is to do a longer review but not as part of the new lesson. For example, you may do the review before recess and teach the lesson after recess. You may do the review the day before. Or, if there are many students in the class who are struggling, you may decide to re-teach the skill.[64]

If you have an intervention program in your school, or in your classroom – where students receive support to allow them access to grade-level content – intervention is the perfect place for extended review. Reviewing, or reteaching, constituent skills immediately before they will be needed for a new lesson is a great use of intervention time. From a student perspective, it is extremely difficult to learn a constituent skill at the same time as you are learning another new skill.

---

63   Tick tock, tick tock.

64   If the performance of a skill is so poor that you believe you need to reteach the lesson, treat both planning and delivery of the reteach as if it were a new lesson. If the students' performance on the skill is as bad as you believe, for all intents and purposes it is a new lesson.

Approximate time to complete: 4-12 minutes

Depending on age of students

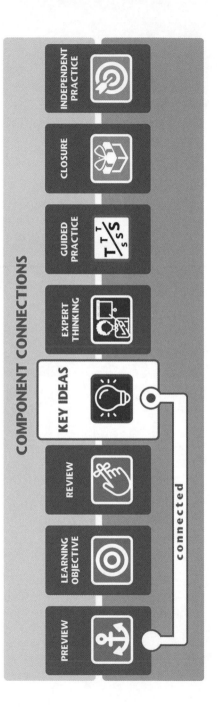

COMPONENT CONNECTIONS

PREVIEW

LEARNING OBJECTIVE

REVIEW

KEY IDEAS

EXPERT THINKING

GUIDED PRACTICE

CLOSURE

INDEPENDENT PRACTICE

connected

CHAPTER 5
KEY IDEAS

Big ideas in key ideas:

- Key ideas is the conceptual part of the lesson.
- Concepts should be taught in every lesson.
- Concepts include both declarative and conditional knowledge.
- Concept maps and language frames are introduced.
- The difference between 'what' and 'how'.

OVERVIEW

A frequent and justified criticism of the standards preceding the common core, was that students were able to perform tasks but had no conceptual understanding of what they were doing. In math, students could perform standard algorithms, which in many cases are simply shortcuts, but could not explain why they worked or why they were being performed. In many cases, students could not explain what they had just done.

Because the learning targets in the prior standards matched high stakes assessments, which in many cases did not require conceptual understanding or problem-solving ability, many concepts were simply not taught. Teachers became very effective at teaching students how to perform well on high stakes testing. Therefore, the concepts that supported the skills were many times entirely omitted from lessons.

Claiming that state or other high stakes assessments do not require students to understand the concepts undergirding algorithms is not a valid excuse for not teaching them. Thankfully, hopefully, the assessments that measure proficiency in the current standards *do* require that students understand, explain, model, and apply concepts to problems or questions.

Students need information organized.

There is so much information available at students' fingertips. Why not just point them in the general direction of websites, videos, primary sources, or heaven forbid, a textbook? Students are lacking two important things that prevent the elimination of teachers and students going straight to other sources to become geniuses. They need basic information about concepts, and they need a structure to help organize that information.

There have been many studies of students' ability to read and comprehend informational text. The main determinant to students' ability to successfully comprehend text is their background knowledge.[65] It does not matter how extensive their vocabulary is. It does not matter what their IQ is. If they have never seen a baseball game, they will not be able to comprehend a book about baseball strategy.

Have you ever attempted to teach students to read a text with care? You may have told students to highlight important details as they read. What did the students do? They created a sea of yellow ... because without knowing the content, they had to make the assumption that everything was important. If everything is important, then nothing is important. If a student does not know the content, she will not know what is important.

During the presentation of key ideas, the teacher will provide enough background information to the students to allow them to begin to cull the non-important from the important. The teacher does this by

---

65   This includes audio and visual media.

telling the story of the concept through presenting the students with an overview.

Even with an overview of the information, as novices students still need the teacher to model how she organizes the information. Information without organization can be overwhelming.

CONCEPTS: DECLARATIVE AND CONDITIONAL

The key ideas component of the FAST Framework is the place where concepts are developed and practiced. It is the difference between students just being able to randomly remember an algorithm from some lesson or assessment and them understanding the concept behind it. Students need to learn what concepts are and when they can be applied.

Declarative knowledge answers the interrogative 'what'. What is a metaphor? What is a theme? What is a quadratic function? What is the periodic table of the elements? The answers to all those questions are part of the content that is taught during key ideas.

Conditional knowledge answers the interrogative 'when'. When would a person encounter this concept in the discipline? When would a person encounter this concept in the world? Stated differently, under what conditions or circumstances would a student encounter this concept? For example, when might you read a metaphor? When would you use a quadratic function? When might there be a demand to use the periodic table? The answer to those questions is content that would also be taught during key ideas.

Conditional knowledge is the conceptual element that is missing from most lessons. Declarative knowledge is not sufficient for students if they are to develop an in-depth understanding of when concepts are applied. If students are to proceed through the learning process to application, conditional knowledge must be included in the conceptual component of the lesson.

The better the students understand the conceptual portion of the lesson, the easier application will be. On the other hand, if students do not understand what the concept is, or when it is used, the teacher is wasting her time teaching students how to perform a skill. If students can answer both of the questions, 'What is it?' and 'When do I use it?', then they are ready to progress to the skill portion of the lesson.

Paradoxically, this does not mean that understanding the concept at a deep, expert level is necessary. The learning objective, which is driven by the grade level of the student, will guide the teacher in the necessary level of understanding. For example, students must understand (i.e. as declarative knowledge) that a metaphor is:

> ... a figure of speech that refers, for rhetorical effect, to one thing by mentioning another thing. It may provide clarity or identify hidden similarities. Usually, the two things mentioned are not similar or related. For example: 'My baby is a monster when she misses her nap'.

However, if students do not understand when a metaphor is frequently used, they will not easily recognize a metaphor when it is being used by an author. Nor will students know when to use a metaphor themselves. There are broadly three instances when a metaphor may be used (i.e. conditional knowledge): (1) to create a picture in a reader's mind, (2) to help a reader understand a concept, and 3) to make writing more interesting.[66] Students must know both 'what' and 'when' before they are able to apply knowledge of metaphors to either reading or writing. But, students do not need a deep, thorough understanding in the initial lesson.[67]

The better a student understands a concept, the easier it will be to master the skill. Even though the skill is developed in the next component of the lesson (i.e. expert thinking), conceptual knowledge is embedded in the skill development of an effective lesson. Students need to learn 'what' before they learn 'how'.

THE DIFFERENCE BETWEEN 'WHAT' AND 'HOW'

Teachers present the 'what' of the lesson in the key ideas component of the FAST Framework. The 'what' is developed by providing definitions,

---

66 See, 'What are three reasons to use metaphors in writing?', *Enotes*. Available at: https://www.enotes.com/homework-help/what-three-reasons-use-metaphors-writings-340271. Are there more than three instances when a metaphor may be used? I am sure there are! However, for the first lesson about a concept the information provided is inflexible, these are the rules.

67 See appendix II, on the Inflexible – Flexible – Application learning progression.

examples, non-examples, etc. of the concept. In the next lesson component (i.e. expert thinking), teachers will model 'how' to perform some skill or task. If the teacher does an effective job modeling, she will embed and use the concepts that are presented in the key ideas. The difference between what the teacher does in key ideas versus what is presented during expert thinking is the difference between presenting a completed example ('what') versus modeling how to construct the example in a step-by-step manner ('how').

A couple of concrete examples make this clearer. Imagine a science class where students create an alluvial fan as a lab activity. Before the teacher explains the step-by-step process of how the students will create an alluvial fan, she first shows them what it looks like. Showing the students what an alluvial fan is very different from explaining the steps they will use to create one. The teacher instructs the students in 'what' before she explains 'how'.

Another example of 'what' before 'how' is writing a haiku. If a teacher were to begin explaining how to construct a haiku without first giving her students an oppertunity to see a haiku, to hear a haiku, to read a haiku, or to analyze a haiku, the students would be lost. That is not to say that they could not follow the teachers step-by-step instructions and create something, but the students would not understand what they had done.

Many teachers with whom we have worked have not been able to make the distinction between presenting an example of what something is, and modeling how something is done.[68] If the distinction is not made and teachers skip presenting an example, they will attempt to present the example while they are modeling. The result is confusion.[69]

Imagine a teacher who does not present an example of a haiku but just begins to model how to write a haiku:

> Okay class I am going to show you how to write a poem called a haiku. Watch me while I write the first line. The first line isn't very long. I think I am going to write, *'The boy went home.'* That isn't a

---

68 The fact they have a difficult time differentiating is the fault of their training.

69 The confusion may eventually be overcome, but the FAST Framework is not based on 'eventually.' Be efficient. Make it easy on the kids. Show the completed example first.

good first line because the first line has to have five syllables and '*The boy went home*' only has four syllables so I have to change that. '*Boys went home early*'...? That's better...

The problem with the example above is that the teacher is attempting to teach what a haiku is at the same time she is attempting to teach how to write one.[70] As the teacher moves back and forth between teaching the 'what' and teaching the 'how' she does neither effectively or efficiently. The more time that is spent with students being confused because of this delivery flaw, the less time students have to practice their new knowledge and skills.

Is this a fatal flaw in the lesson delivery? Many teachers have overcome presenting new lessons in the exact manner above with students successfully knowing what a haiku is and writing one. Thankfully teacher miscues during a lesson are never fatal, nor do they need to be final. However, they do make it more difficult for students than it needs to be. They extend the time it takes for the students to learn the material. When learning is difficult many students feel like *they* are the problem.[71]

In any discipline, skills can only be applied to concepts. Understanding a concept is a prerequisite to teaching the application of that concept. Students need to learn 'what' before they can efficiently learn 'how'. This statement applies as much to micro learning, such as in a discrete lesson, as to macro learning, like the synthesis of topics and skills in a culminating investigation.

Do not demand that students apply, create, or solve problems prior to them being able to identify concepts and distinguish degrees of quality. Identifying has been given a bad rap as teachers are expected to ask students higher-level questions.[72]

---

70 This usually manifests when the teacher is modeling for the students and she stops and says, 'Wait. I forgot to tell you something you need to know'.

71 When learning is difficult many students may be led to believe it is because they have not developed 'a growth mindset'; or maybe they do not have enough 'grit'.

72 Many teachers have related that during observation by an administrator or coach they have received the feedback that they should be asking higher-level questions during their lessons. This feedback has been given even in contexts when the lessons in question were early in the teaching sequence (see appendix II).

Imagine a lesson in which students are given multiple geological formations and asked to:

- Identify geological features in the formations that may or may not be an alluvial fan.
- Provide the reasons for their decisions which must include the characteristics of an alluvial fan.

No one could say those tasks are not cognitively engaging. However, if the students have not understood the concept of an alluvial fan then they will not be successful in identifying one. All too often teachers are in a hurry to get students to produce something before they understand what they are being asked to produce.

English language arts example ('what before how')

My colleague related to me an example of the power of 'what before how'. An English language arts teacher had explained to my colleague that her students just could not understand how to compose a well written statement that explained an author's message.[73] The teacher had laid out posters with the steps for writing about the author's message. She had provided language frames for each step. She told my colleague that they had been repeatedly going over this in class. Yet, her 3rd grade students were still continuing to provide one- or two-word answers despite her thinking it had been made clear that she wanted them to use detailed and thoughtful sentences. The teacher was pretty discouraged, but she wanted to revisit writing about author's messages one more time.

My colleague asked her how she recognizes when a student has correctly identified the topic. She then asked her how she recognizes when a student has correctly written a good statement about an author's message. The teacher began to list the attributes of both. My colleague explained that these were what she would present to her class as the key ideas!

At the time, my colleague suspected that what prevented the students from delivering what the teacher wanted was a lack of clarity regarding some key conceptual details. Specifically, the students did not have clear criteria for writing an effective statement about the author's message. The

---

73   This example was related to me by my colleague Carin Contreras.

students were not clear on what an effective statement about the author's message 'looked like'.

My colleague explained to the teacher that the real focus of the key ideas component of the lesson they were planning was 'what' an effective statement of the author's message looked like. For example, it was important to make it clear to the students that while a statement of the topic was only a few words at most, the author's message by contrast should be written as a complete sentence that included specific information and used precise vocabulary.

The teacher decided to present these key ideas about the author's message, and provide students ample practice identifying effective statements. Only after students demonstrated their ability to accurately identify effective statements of authors' messages would she proceed to the next lesson component, (i.e. expert thinking) modeling 'how' they would create their own statements about the text they were reading.

When the teacher presented the key ideas of what was included in an effective statement of author's message, she was clear and to the point. It was so elegantly simple. However, it was when she gave the students time to practice distinguishing between the two that her teacher-craft really shone through. She gave the students physical gestures they could use to indicate whether it was a topic, an 'ok' author's message, or a 'really good' author's message. She also provided the same language frame she had used earlier in the unit for the students to explain their reasoning. Through maybe 15 quick examples, a few of each kind of choice, she provided the students with ample practice of both the key ideas and the key vocabulary.

Practice	Student Response (Notice Language Frames)
a) Magnets are fun.	This is an ok author's message because it doesn't use descriptive language. (Hands on hips)
b) Magnets	This is a topic because it is only one word. (Hands on head)
c) Magnets can be found in many places in your house.	This is a really good author's message because it is a complete sentence and it uses descriptive language. (Hands in air)
a) It is important to be truthful because people will trust you, especially when you need them.	This is a really good author's message because it is a complete sentence and it uses specific language. (Hands in air)
b) It is good to be truthful.	This is an ok author's message because it is vague. (Hands on hips)
c) Honesty	This is a topic because it is only one word. (Hands on head)

Of course, from the back of the room my colleague was celebrating the teacher's victory because the presentation and checking for understanding of the key ideas were so well done. And if they had any doubt as to whether the students appreciated the clarity the lesson had provided, one student helpfully exclaimed, 'This is such a fun game!' The enthusiasm for this 'game' the teacher had taught them carried into the students eventual practice writing and evaluating their own statements of the author's message.

When students are given ample practice identifying and explaining key ideas using purposeful examples, they are more confident when producing their own to the teacher's criteria. Identification and evaluation should always precede production.

Math example ('what before how')

Let's now look at a successfully executed example which also demonstrates the importance of 'what before how'. While I was planning a math lesson with a 5th grade teacher on determining the volume of rectangular prisms and cubes, we approached the key ideas portion of the lesson with the goal of defining volume (declarative knowledge), identifying the type of objects that have volume (conditional knowledge), and then analyzing the use of the formula $V=l \times w \times h$ to determine volume.

In defining volume, the teacher referred to constructed paper cubes and rectangular prisms that the students had made the day before. She then brought the students back to the preview of the lesson, 'Remember at the beginning of the lesson when I asked you, "What do you think is inside this rectangular prism?" and you replied, "Nothing...air!" and I told you that in this lesson, you would learn that volume is what's inside?' The students all nodded.

She instructed them to pick up either their cube or rectangular prism and imagine if they opened up the top. She then showed them a centimeter cube and asked, 'Do you think we could fill up this 3-dimensional shape with centimeter cubes?' All the students agreed.

'If we had a bigger rectangular prism, could we fill it up with one inch cubes?' The students nodded. If we had a really big rectangular prism, could we fill it up with meter sized cubes?' The students replied, 'Yes!'

The teacher then established a definition of volume (i.e. 'what'): 'The amount of space that an object occupies is volume.' The students replied, 'Ohhhhh!'. However, the learning objective also included using the formula $V=l\times w\times h$ to calculate the volume of rectangular prisms and cubes (i.e. 'why'). The teacher referred to this slide and directed the students to read the formula aloud with her:

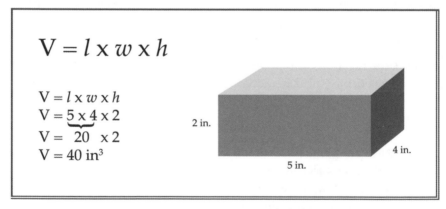

She then asked the students to share what they thought each letter represented by turning to their partner and explaining. 'V represents volume', 'W represents width', and so on. She then picked four students to share out to confirm. She proceeded to ask questions of the students to guide them through the analysis of the already completed representation of using the formula for volume to determine the volume of rectangular prisms and cubes.

Students observed and recognized that they would use the order of operations to solve the multiplication problem (i.e. $V=5\times4\times2=40^3$). When they arrived at the solution, the teacher asked, 'Why is the solution cubed?' (i.e. 40^3). Using their flexible thinking around volume and 3 dimensional shapes they were able to make the connection: 'It's because it's the volume of a 3-dimensional shape, so it has to be cubed, like the cubes filling the prism!'

In the key ideas section of this math lesson, declarative knowledge was developed by answering the question, '*What* is volume?' The concept of volume was understood by the students because the teacher successfully related the idea to a concrete experience that students had shared (i.e. building rectangular prisms and cubes out of paper and filling them up with centimeter cubes). Students quickly grasped the declarative knowledge and were able to move to the conditional. The calculation of volume is used when determining what is 'inside' a three-dimensional object. It answers the demand, 'How do I determine the volume of a rectangular prism or cube?' The teacher then connected the students' prior knowledge of formulas for two dimensional figures, to the new formula for volume.

All students engaged in the analysis of a completed mathematical procedure to make sense of the demand and to break down both the 'what' and the 'how' of a successfully completed solution. Through intentional teaching of the key ideas in this lesson, students had enough opportunity to learn both the declarative and conditional knowledge needed to be ready for the teacher's expert thinking (modeling). Reflecting on the lesson, the teacher shared that she appreciated the concise purpose and design for its key ideas. 'The pace of my lesson is so much better when I design exactly what to focus on in the key ideas. Without it, I tend to jump ahead in my teaching to information the students don't need to know yet!' Success!

DEVELOPING CONCEPTS

Concepts are developed through an easily repeatable process. First, new concepts are developed by connecting them to students' prior knowledge from the preview (or prior lessons). Next, a definition of the new concept is provided. Examples and non-examples are provided. And finally, teachers must provide immediate practice.[74] Let's look in detail at each part of that process.

Connecting to preview

We learn by making connections and seeking patterns. The preview connects students' prior knowledge to new concepts. Many times students are familiar with concepts, but do not know their academic name (see chapter 2).

Define in context and include multiple criteria

Definitions should always be provided in context. In context simply means in conjunction with a very clear example that is related to the prior lesson components and will match subsequent ones. Coherent, consistent lessons provide continuity of clear examples. A denotative definition of an academic term that is not delivered in context usually creates more confusion than clarity. For example, can you imagine a student searching for the definition of an extended metaphor and finding this on *Wikipedia*:

> An extended metaphor, also known as a conceit or sustained metaphor, is an author's use of a single metaphor or analogy at length through multiple linked tenors, vehicles, and grounds throughout a poem or story.

This definition appears prominently on the first page of search results of a google search for 'extended metaphor'. When the student enentered their search there was only one term they did not know ('extended metaphor'). Now they are wondering, 'What are "conceits", "tenors", "vehicles", and "grounds"?'.[75]

---

74   Immediate practice includes informal assessments such as checking for understanding questions and tasks.

75   One of the most frequently observed ineffective and inefficient teaching practices is the introduction of definitions of key concepts prior to the lesson. A common practice is assigning a list of 'vocabulary words' for students to define prior to the lesson by looking the terms up in glossaries, dictionaries, and/or online sources. Most teachers will describe this as introducing the critical vocabulary so the students can better understand the lesson because they are more familiar with the specialized vocabulary. This is rarely effective because students often do not understand the definitions given.

Better, more useful, definitions define at least two criteria or critical elements. A better definition of a metaphor is:

A figure of speech in which a word or phrase is used to describe an object or action which is not literally applicable.

In this definition of metaphor there are two distinct components that can be used by a student to determine if a figure of speech is in fact a metaphor. First, the word must be applied to an object or action, and second, the work or phrase is not to be taken literally.

Example of identifying a metaphor using multiple criteria:

'His fingers were leafless twigs.'

Criteria #1. An object is described – fingers.

Criteria #2. The description is not literal – the man's fingers were not really twigs.

Language frame

The man's fingers are being described as twigs. Fingers are not twigs. Because both criteria were met, this is a metaphor.

Non-example a metaphor using multiple criteria:

'His fingers were bony.'

Criteria #1. An object is described – fingers.

Criteria #2. The description is literal.

Language frame

The man's fingers are being described as bones. Fingers have bones. Because both criteria were not met, this is not a metaphor.

Having at least two criteria demands more critical thought in order to determine that a phrase is actually a metaphor. Each phrase must contain both criteria to satisfy the requirements of the definition. If an example does not contain all the criteria, it is not the thing being studied.

Another example of a concept using at least two criteria or critical elements:

Germ: A very small living thing that causes disease.

This example has three criteria: (1) small, (2) living, and (3) causes disease.

Q: Is a virus a germ?

A: A virus is small, it is not living, and it causes disease. Because it does not meet all three criteria it is not a germ.

Use clear examples

The selection of examples is critical. When teaching initial lessons about new concepts, the type of understanding that is being sought is inflexible: examples must fit the definitions exactly.[76] Initial lessons are not the time to introduce all the possible variations that a student may encounter. As discussed in chapter 1, when teaching initial lessons *all examples must match exactly* to whatever has been presented. Inflexible understanding precedes flexible understanding.

Clear examples during initial instruction are easy to understand. Clear examples appear simple because they are clear. Clear examples have been stripped of distractions that may confuse kids.[77] Teachers often are hesitant to provide clear simple examples because students will not be assessed using such simple examples.

Non-examples

While learning what something is, an example alone is sometimes not enough to make a concept clear. We all learn by comparing and contrasting new information with known information. Non-examples can provide students with clarity of concepts by providing a contrast. Adding what something is not – a non-example – can help make the concept clearer.

When using non-examples there are two important considerations. First, the non-examples should be clearly non-examples. The clarity of non-examples should match the clarity of the examples and be directly related to those examples. In the class describing metaphors discussed above

---

76   See appendix II.

77   Have you ever seen a picture of a girl eating an ice cream cone that it is supposed to be an example of 'dessert'. Some children may think the girl is 'dessert'; or her dress is 'dessert'.

both the example and the non-example use a description of fingers, as either 'twigs' (example) or 'bony' (non-example).[78] Second, only use non-examples when they further understanding. In the younger grades (K, 1st, and sometimes 2nd) students may not have prior experience with some basline concepts, limiting their understanding of the new concept itself. If this is the case, non-examples do not help clarify, and instead only serve to confuse. As much as examples can elucidate, non-example can extinguish understanding with younger students.

When non-examples are not appropriate, practice with lots and lots of examples is a must.

Immediate practice

In the section above on including multiple criteria in definitions, there were several examples of identifying metaphors and germs. Asking students to answer questions focused on criteria like this provides immediate practice for students. It also provides teachers with data to inform their instruction. Using the answers from the students the teacher can answer, 'Can I move on? Or, do the students need more practice?'

IMPORTANT!

It has been said that if you really want to learn something, you should teach it. The inverse of that is, if you don't know something, you can't teach it.[79] Knowing a concept, in this context, includes being able to clearly articulate what the concept is using all the strategies listed above. We have observed many lessons in which the teacher provides explanations and definitions of a concept that change slightly with each iteration. Students need exact language that is replicated many times during the lesson.[80] It is this exact language that is the genesis of the language frame that students will use during the lesson.

---

78 Children can be very literal and become confused easily. If 'The woman's hair was silk' was given as an example of a metaphor and 'The statue's hands were stone' was given as a non-example, then some children might easily think that soft things can be metaphors and hard things can not.

79 It is either the inverse, converse, or corollary. I always get them mixed up. But you get the idea.

80 This is especially important during a lesson when teaching in inflexible concepts (see appendix II).

Let's look at an example of the importance of knowing content before designing a lesson. An 8th grade language arts teacher joined me to plan a lesson she was going to teach the next day. When I asked what she was planning to teach she referred to her pacing guide and said, 'It looks like tomorrow I am supposed to be teaching "parallel structure".'

In my customary fashion, modeling how to think about focused lesson design, I asked, 'What about parallel structure?'

Continuing to look at the pacing guide, the teacher responded, 'This is the first lesson so they will "identify parallel structure in writing".'

'Okay, good.' I continued with the planning, 'Now that we know what the students are supposed to do with parallel structure, let's define "parallel structure".' I looked at the teacher with pen in hand ready to write and asked, 'How do you want to define it? What is parallel structure?'

After a minute or so of looking through her pacing guide, the teacher shrugged her shoulders, and only a little embarrassed, said. 'I don't know.' 'Well let's find out,' I said. An important part of coaching for me is to model how to design a lesson. That includes modeling what to do when you don't know something. The teacher Googled parallel structure. The definition below is similar to what we found.

> **Parallel structure** (also called parallelism) is the repetition of a chosen grammatical form within a sentence. By making each compared item or idea in your sentence follow the same grammatical pattern, you create a parallel construction.[81]

The teacher, after reading the definition, looked at me, cocked her head like the old RCA Victor dog, and said, 'What?'

'I know, right,' trying to comfort. Still in the modeling mode, I suggested we look at some of the examples and non-examples provided in the link.

Example: Joe likes singing, walking, and swimming.

Non Example: Joe likes singing, walking, to swim.

---

81   See 'Paralell Structure', *Evergreen Writing Center*. Available at: https://www.evergreen.edu/writingcenter/handouts/grammar/parallel.pdf.

Example: She likes to swim, to sing, and to jump.

Non-Example: She likes swimming, singing, and to jump.[82]

After looking at several examples, she understood what was meant by 'a chosen grammatical construction' she looked at me, smiled, and said, 'Got it! I know how to teach this.'

Providing a definition to students is not sufficient when teaching concepts. If all we needed to understand concepts were definitions, we would not need textbooks. All we would need is dictionaries. Clear examples give clarity to definitions. Clear examples not only provide clarity on what a concept is and when to use it, they can also illustrate how to develop the procedure to apply the concept.

DESIGN TIPS

Tip #1. Use Whole – Part – Whole Structure
The vast majority of the population prefer to start learning by seeing the 'whole picture'. Start with the big picture first. Then identify discrete parts. And finally, return to the big picture.[83] Think of a jigsaw puzzle. If you were to instruct someone on putting together a jigsaw puzzle the first thing you would do is show them the picture of the completed puzzle. Then you would look for details within the picture and even within the structure of the puzzle itself: things like corners, edges, bright colors, etc. And finally, you would check back with the picture on the box to see that the pieces are creating the big picture. Whole – Part – Whole.

Tip #1a. Whole (tell the story)
Start by telling the 'story' of whatever concept you are teaching. What is the story? It is a brief overview and description of the concept. This brief story is the first 'whole' of the Whole – Part – Whole structure. The story will include a definition of the concept, 'what' it is. What is the story of metaphors? Why do writers use them? Why do readers like them?

What is the story of germs? What is the story of complementary angles? What is the story of fractions? What is the story of stories? There is always

---

82   See Mary Gormandy White, 'Paralell Structures', *YourDictionary*. Available at: http://examples.yourdictionary.com/parallel-structure-examples.html.

83   The Whole – Part – Whole structure will be discussed again in chapter 8.

a story. When I describe the story to teachers, I tell them to think of the initial part of a *Wikipedia* entry. There is always a concise overview of the topic in just a few paragraphs or lines. That is the story. Imagine a lesson with the following objective: Students will write an essay describing a family in a poverty trap using the concept of the cycle of poverty. Here is an abridged version of the *Wikipedia* entry for the 'cycle of poverty':

> In economics, a **poverty trap** or **cycle of poverty** is caused by self-reinforcing mechanisms that cause poverty. Once it exists, it will continue unless there is outside intervention, and can persist across generations. Families trapped in the cycle of poverty, have either limited or no resources. There are many disadvantages that collectively work in a circular process making it virtually impossible for individuals to break this cycle, such as lack of access to financial capital, education, or social connections. In other words, impoverished individuals often do not posess the economic and social resources required to escape their own poverty. This could mean that the poor remain poor throughout their lives.

Tip #1b. Part (provide details)
The story provides an overview of the content, but it lacks details, examples, and non-examples. Those are the next parts that will be provided. In this example, we could sketch out the details of the poverty cycle as follows. A child grows up in poverty. They have a disadvantaged education. Because of poor education, they struggle to get a good job. Without a good job the family stays in poverty. The cycle returns to the child in poverty.

Tip #1c. Choose a concept map to provide details
A concept map is a visual representation of the story.[84] Choose the concept map that best represents the story you are telling. This story tells you which map to use: the *Wikipedia* article tells us the story of the cycle of poverty. In this case the concept map that depicts a cycle is the obvious choice.

---

84 In declarative lessons the concept map is also an important part of expert thinking as the two components are combined. The only six maps you will need to choose from are in appendix I.

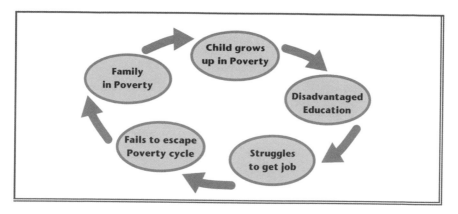

Is it really always that easy to choose a concept map? With practice, yes, it is.

Because the story is an overview, a big picture, there are very few details included. The details that will populate the concept map are the parts. The concept map provides a visual form for the 'part' component of the Whole – Part – Whole structure.

Here is another example: teaching the five senses to primary students. What is the story? We have five senses, or five ways we experience the world. They are *hearing, touch, sight, taste,* and *smell.* Each of these senses is a tool your brain uses to help you build a clear picture of your world.

The organs involved in your five senses are:

- Ears (hearing).
- Skin (touch).
- Eyes (sight).
- Tongue (taste).
- Nose (smell).

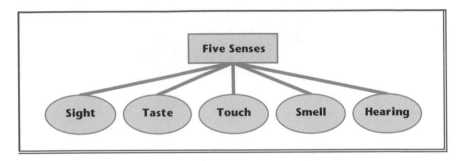

The text of the story will give you the biggest clues as to which concept map to use. Populating the concept map with details provides the parts.

Tip #2. Design a language frame that matches the concept map

Language frame for the generational poverty cycle concept map above:

I know that if a child _____ it is likely she _____ .

I know that if a child <u>grows up in poverty</u>, it is likely that she <u>will get a poor education</u>.

I know that if a child <u>gets a poor education</u>, it is likely that she <u>will not get a good job</u>.[85]

Tip #3. Use consistent and precise language

There are many times in our lives when in conversation we may say things slightly differently and the person to whom we are speaking has no problem in understanding the meaning of what we are saying. This is because of shared prior knowledge and colloquial language. However, when in the classroom, if you described a family in poverty as 'hitting bottom', or saying they 'can't make ends meet', you may have some confused students.

Tip #4. Use academic language

Use the proper names of concepts. Use academic language: the language of the discipline you are teaching. Have faith in your ability to teach any given concept and the academic term that names it. The first-time students

---

85   Note that these language frames are using multi-criteria definitions.

encounter a new concept it literally does not matter what you name it. A teacher could call a metaphor a 'gongson' and it would not change the ease or difficulty of learning the concept for students.[86] Both the words 'metaphor' and 'gongson' are words the students do not know.

The argument that proper academic language is too difficult for students was addressed in chapter 3. Anything that has not yet been taught seems difficult. Once students learn the concept, any label that names that concept will not be difficult.

Tip #5. Prepare checking for understanding questions

It is easy to come up with lower level questions on the spot. What is not easy is coming up with higher level questions that require students to become more cognitively engaged with the content.

DELIVERY TIPS

Tip #1. Pay attention to your OWL

Depending on the age of your students you have 4-10 minutes to deliver the key ideas component of the lesson. It is always better to teach a smaller chunk and have time to practice than it is to attempt to teach too much and have no time to practice.

Using concept maps helps to reach more natural places to stop. In the example above, the five senses, you may have originally planned to present all five senses. As you get into the lesson you realize you will not have time to complete all five, you may just present and practice three of the senses.

Leave sufficient time to practice.

Tip #2. Check for understanding regularly

You should be checking for understanding with the appropriate level of questions every 2-4 minutes. If students do not understand content at a level that is satisfactory to you, then there is less material to review than if you had delivered content for 7-10 minutes before checking for understanding.

---

86 'Gongson' is an invented word.

Tip #3. Demand students use the language frames

All students should use the language frames. The language frames, if constructed properly, not only reinforce the concept but allow students to fluently express complex ideas using proper academic vocabulary. This is achieved by decreasing the cognitive load on the linguistic component of the task (i.e. the extraneous load), and increasing the germane cognitive load on the targeted concept. Each time a student uses the language frame to answer a checking for understanding question she is practicing and reinforcing the new concept.

All students should use the language frames. Frequently teachers ask if it is necessary for students who are able to articulate concepts without the use of language frames to use them. The answer is 'yes'. Using language frames is not detrimental to anyone. I suggest teachers use the following script if a student asks to respond in their own words.

Student: 'Is it okay if I say it my own way, in my own words?'

Teacher: 'Of course it is. But you need to use the language frame first.'

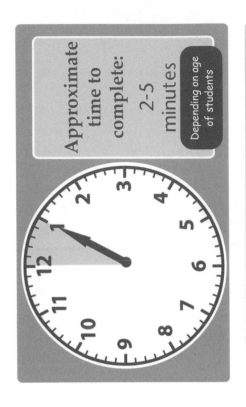

Approximate time to complete: 2-5 minutes

Depending on age of students

COMPONENT CONNECTIONS

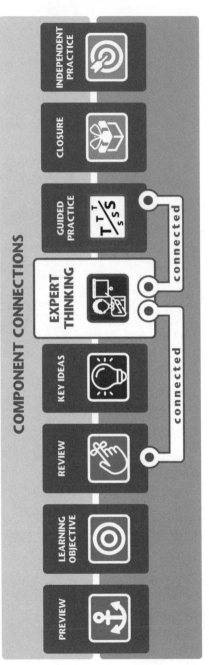

PREVIEW

LEARNING OBJECTIVE

REVIEW

KEY IDEAS

EXPERT THINKING

GUIDED PRACTICE

CLOSURE

INDEPENDENT PRACTICE

connected

connected

connected

CHAPTER 6
EXPERT THINKING

Big ideas in expert thinking:

- Expert thinking is modeling.
- Modeling is the first of the two biggest time savers.
- Modeling looks different for declarative and procedural lessons.
- Model two examples.
- Use the Whole – Part – Whole structure.

This chapter explains one the biggest timesavers in the FAST Framework. Modeling in the manner prescribed can reduce the amount of time it takes by more than 75%.

OVERVIEW: EXPERT THINKING AND MAKING THINKING VISIBLE

Many, many years ago I was sitting in a class fulfilling requirements for a teaching credential. The professor, a well-loved, popular icon in the department said, 'Modeling is the most powerful method of teaching. But don't use me as an example.' At the time, he did not appear to be attempting irony. What is my evidence? Number one, no one in the class laughed. Just because no one laughed does not mean the professor did not intend the statement to be funny. Number two, an experienced and beloved professor, one who must have gotten his share of laughs over the years, would have had the comedic skill set to let his audience know he just told a joke that bombed ('Is this mike on?'). But there was no admission that the statement was meant to be taken other than at face value. Ironic or not, the professor was right. Modeling is the most powerful method of teaching. But not all modeling is equal. Modeling is most powerful when done well.

In our attempt to keep instruction as artful as possible, there is little in the FAST Framework that is prescribed. Expert thinking, or modeling, is an exception.[87] There are many ineffective and inefficient ways to model, and a limited number of efficient and effective ways. In order to eliminate as many ineffective and inefficient practices as possible, there will be more sample scripts, more warnings, and more examples in this chapter.

THIS IS THE LONGEST CHAPTER IN *TEACHING FAST*

This is also one of the most important chapters. It may also differ most from what you currently believe about effective modeling. Modeling in the FAST Framework is structured and efficient (i.e. fast).

The design and delivery of procedural lessons and declarative lessons differ slightly from one another when you are implementing the FAST Framework. Because the difference is knowable, learnable, and teachable there is only one FAST Framework. There are many designers of lesson plan templates who think that teaching concepts is so different from teaching skills that they go to the trouble of designing two or more types of lesson templates.[88] The reality is that what makes procedural and declarative lessons different is much less than what makes them similar. It

---

87 Reminder: expert thinking is modeling. Who is the expert to whom we are referring? YOU! The teacher.

88 I once skimmed a book on lesson plan design that proposed teachers should learn five different lesson designs.

is more simple to learn, understand, and master one framework, than it is to master several.

Because procedural lessons and declarative lessons are more alike than they are different, both will be covered in this chapter. Cognitive scientists teach us it is better to learn one thing at a time when two concepts or skills are closely related. Therefore, this chapter will be divided into two sections: procedural and declarative. Because there is so much overlap between the two, readers may find explanations that appear in both sections.

IMPORTANT CONSIDERATIONS DURING EXPERT THINKING

If the senses were ranked in order of importance for learning and remembering, vision would stand out as number one. In any sort of explanation of expert thinking, or modeling, a visual example is the most powerful and should always be included.[89] Modeling, which is a visual representation of a teacher's expert thinking, is critical to making learning accessible to all students. This applies to both procedural lessons and declarative lessons.

It is important for teachers to identify whether the lesson they intend to teach is procedural or declarative before beginning to design the lesson.[90] There may be minor differences in the design and delivery in several of the components, but one of the most obvious differences is evident during modeling.

The next two sections provide further clarifications about how those differences will manifest in the two types of lessons. Procedural lessons will be examined first as they fit best into a common understanding of modeling.

---

89   This statement in no way refers to VAK learning tyles, an unproven, yet enduring, theory about how students learn.

90   See appendix IV.

PROCEDURAL LESSONS

Designing a procedure

As the name implies, during procedural lessons the teacher's goal is to model for students how to perform new skills using a step-by-step procedure.[91] Many folks in education think of algorithms as being limited to math. Actually, algorithms are used by experts in all disciplines and fields; academic as well as practical. Think about all the tasks that computers can be programmed to perform. Computers can be programmed to write a novel, to analyze rocks, to write music. What is the implication of that? Someone wrote code for all those programs. What is code? It is an algorithm, a procedure, a series of steps and instructions.

According to a report I read many years ago, the vast majority of math lessons are procedural in nature, i.e. they use an algorithm, or procedural steps to perform a skill. The same report stated that most language arts lessons could be taught using an algorithm. It is difficult to argue against the observation that the vast majority of skills taught to students in math, language arts, social studies, science, physical education, the arts, etc. can be performed following some step-by-step procedure.

Examples of procedures

Example #1. A math teacher is teaching a procedural lesson with the learning objective: subtracting a one-digit number from a two-digit number using regrouping. The teacher will model this skill to the class as a procedure, 'Students, when I subtract a single digit number from a two-digit number, the first thing I do is ...'. The procedure is the step-by-step process an expert uses to solve such a problem. Below are the steps a teacher might present to a class:[92]

Sample problem - $\begin{array}{r} 13 \\ -\ 6 \end{array}$

---

91 The terms algorithms, steps, and procedures will be used interchangeably.

92 Important! If a step in the procedure is to regroup, the students must have been taught to regroup in a prior lesson.

Step 1: Analyze – sufficient number of ones to subtract?[93]

Step 2: Regroup – if necessary.

Step 3: Subtract.

Step 4: Is answer reasonable?

These steps are the procedure that the teacher would use if she were to solve this type of problem. Having a list of steps available provides a map for students to follow as problems are modeled by the teacher. An expert will use the algorithm to solve problems of this type. However, merely listing the steps to solve a problem is not modeling. A teacher shares her expert thinking when she uses the steps to solve problems and makes her thinking known (see the sample scripts later in this section).

Example #2. An ELA teacher is teaching a procedural lesson with the learning objective: interpreting metaphors. The procedure, or expert thinking, the teacher presents to the class might be as follows:

The teacher provides a sample metaphor:

My <u>baby is a monster</u> when she doesn't sleep.[94]

Step 1: Analyze – is the underlined phrase figurative language? are two things being compared?[95]

Step 2: Identify what is being described.

Step 3: Identify what this 'thing' is being compared to?

Step 4: What are the characteristics of the point of comparison in step 3.

Step 5: Apply those characteristics to what is being described.

The use of steps to interpret metaphors provides a map for the students as the teacher makes her thinking visible.

---

93 The analysis is an application of the concepts and conditions taught during key ideas in this lesson or a prior lesson.

94 In this example lesson, because the skill being taught is interpreting metaphors, the metaphors are identified for the students. Identifying metaphors is a different skill, taught during a previous lesson.

95 The analysis is an application of the concepts and conditions taught during key ideas in this lesson or a prior lesson.

DESIGNING PROCEDURE: MATHEMATICS

Elementary teachers report that designing math procedures, aka steps, are relatively easy. Ask any elementary teacher how to perform long division and they will say something like, 'The first thing you do is ... And then what you do is ... Next you ... Finally you ...'.[96] Most of us already think about math algorithms in terms of steps. Many algorithms have been taught in a similar manner for generations.[97] Most math textbooks include procedures for both teachers and students. Solving example problems using a procedure is the essence of modeling in a procedural lesson.

Is there any difference between the algorithms that have been used for hundreds of years and the steps a teacher should use while modeling for her students? The answer is yes, at least initially. Initially procedures may include additional steps that will reinforce concepts and conditions that will not be necessary after students master the algorithms.

A valid criticism of just teaching students algorithms is that students do not understand the concepts that allow these shortcuts to work. For generations most of what was traditionally taught in elementary math classes was essentially shortcuts with no conceptual underpinning. For example, do you remember how to divide a fraction by a fraction? Of course, you do: simply invert and multiply. Do you know why inverting and multiplying works? Do you care why it works?[98]

When modeling, teachers must explain to students why the procedure has been selected. This is why this component is named, 'expert thinking' versus simply modeling.

Teaching only the algorithms without conceptual understanding and application was identified in the previous chapter as a major factor in the genesis of the common core standards.[99] All procedures *must* have their conceptual underpinning embedded. The key ideas in the new lesson *must*

---

96   As stated in a previous chapter, elementary teachers seem to have a more difficult time teaching key ideas or concepts.

97   We have been using the same algorithms for generations because they worked in the 18th century, and they continue to work in the 21st century.

98   'Mine is not to reason why, simply invert and multiply.' A traditional math ditty about dividing fractions.

99   It was also the main impetus for the development of the 'New Math' of the 1960s.

include the concept and conditions for its application. If mathematical concepts are not embedded in the steps being taught the students are only being provided directions for performing shortcuts. Well designed procedures have the concepts taught in the key ideas embedded in them.

In the math example above, the embedded concepts in the steps are place value and equivalent forms of representing numbers. For example: 13 = 1 ten and 3 ones = 13 ones. These two concepts are what a student needs to know in order to understand why regrouping works.

DESIGNING PROCEDURES: ENGLISH LANGUAGE ARTS

In contrast to math where procedures are easily constructed, most language arts teachers, which includes all elementary teachers, have a much more difficult time creating procedures for many language skills. The reason for this is very simple. Fluent speakers perform tasks without having to think about the process.[100] Fluent speakers have already reached a level of automaticity that grants them the gift of performing without conscious thought. Automaticity is a desired state because tasks can be performed with limited conscious cognitive engagement thereby 'freeing space' in working memory for new concepts or skills.

If you ask most elementary school teachers how they find the main idea of a paragraph, they cannot tell you. If you were to push further and ask, 'You can find the main idea of a paragraph, right?' They acknowledge with certitude that they can, but many cannot articulate how they actually find the main idea.[101]

---

100 Ironically, the best support for teaching English language arts skills can be found in English language development (ELD) textbooks. ELD books operate on the assumption that students do not have constituent skills to perform task and must therefore be taught. Many textbooks for fluent English speakers make the opposite assumption and because of that often fall short supporting teachers in lesson design.

101 During a training session I once asked teachers how they determined the main idea of a paragraph. From more than a few primary teachers I got the response, 'I read the paragraph and look for repeated words. Then I count to see which word was used most frequently and I know what the main idea is.' They knew they could find the main idea, but they did not know how they did it. If you don't know how something is done, it is difficult to teach others.

The problem is not that teachers do not know procedures for skills in language arts, most of them have simply never thought about language arts skills as algorithms. Paradoxically, the gift of fluency and automaticity has robbed them of having to think about how they perform many tasks in the language arts.[102]

'DISCOVERING' STEPS IN LANGUAGE ARTS

As stated previously, most English language arts lessons could be taught using algorithms, yet most English language arts texts do not provide procedures for students to learn new skills. Because many teachers, due to their fluency, cannot think of procedures easily on their own, they conclude that no procedures exist. Here are a couple of tips to help teachers discover and articulate procedures for skills they already possess. These tips work for any content area.

A prerequisite for writing steps is a deep understanding of the concepts that are foundational to the skill you will be teaching.[103] In other words, you must know the content!

When discovering steps it helps to remember that there is a hierarchy in language arts as it relates to learning and application. The one language arts application that demonstrates competence in all the other domains is writing. All other skills such as grammar, reading, etc. lead to, or support, writing. We can use that knowledge – that writing is the master of the domain (with a tip of the hat and apologies to Seinfeld) – to discover steps to find the main idea of a paragraph.

When learning to write a paragraph, students are taught very early that each paragraph should contain a strong topic sentence. The topic sentence, the students are taught, tells the reader what the upcoming paragraph is about, as well as determining the structure of the paragraph. The topic

---

102 As I am working with a teacher designing a lesson, when we get to expert thinking I always ask, 'How do you do this problem?' When the teacher responds, 'First I tell the students to …' I abruptly stop her and repeat my question, 'I am not asking you what you are going to tell your students. I am asking how *you* solve the problem.'

103 In this case, a deep understanding means understanding at a level that is at least two grade levels higher than the teacher is currently teaching. Teachers must know the general curriculum demand that their students will face in the future so that the content can be taught in the proper context.

sentence is usually the first sentence in the paragraph, but not always. After the topic sentence, there are sentences that provide supporting details. And, then finally, there is usually some type of wrap up sentence. If students are taught about how to write using this procedure, then it follows that reading materials should follow the same structure. When students are taught how to write, they should be taught the relationship between the procedure for writing and the procedure for reading.

'Great! But what are the steps? Tell me how to discover the steps!'

Option #1. Watch someone, e.g. a colleague, performing the task you will be teaching your students, in this case how to find the main idea of a paragraph. Then ask the person who is performing this task what she was thinking as she performed each task. This is sometimes also known as 'teacher talk', or thinking out loud.

You will have witnessed the colleague perform the task, i.e. the skill, in a step-by-step manner. Because you can already automatically perform the task, it will be easy to identify the procedure the colleague used.

Below is a sample paragraph. Imagine a colleague reading this paragraph while she kept in mind the simple rules of *writing* a paragraph.

Example #1.

> It is important to remember that while such new technology eliminates some jobs, it also creates others. Think about the worker who once fastened bolts on the assembly line. This person might learn how to run and repair the machine that does that job now. Workers of the future must be willing to learn new skills as fast as technology changes. It is one way to ensure the best chances of having a job.[104]

After reading the paragraph your colleague makes this statement regarding the main idea of the paragraph:

> If I wanted to find the main idea of the paragraph the first thing I would do is find the topic sentence. I know the first sentence is usually the topic sentence so I will read that sentence carefully. "It is important to remember that while such new technology eliminates some jobs, it also creates others."

104 *Pacemaker Economics* (2001) Globe Fearon, Upsaddle River, NKL, p. 119.

This text structure looks like proposition and support. When I continue to read the paragraph, I will be looking for examples of job losses and job gains because of technology. Sure enough there are examples of those very things. So, I am going to say that the main idea of the paragraph is that technology makes some jobs obsolete but technology also creates new jobs that had not previously existed.

Option #2. Ask a colleague to watch you perform a skill. Describe what you are doing as you perform the skill. You are not teaching the colleague how to do the skill, you are merely explaining what you are doing as you perform the skill. After watching the skill performed several times, the colleague will be able to report what she saw you do.

The description of what you did should be articulated in the following manner: 'First I saw you do this. Next, I saw you do that. Then I saw you do this. And finally, you finished by doing this.' After she has completed relating all the steps that she saw you perform, you then confirm that this was in fact the procedure you used. Voila! You have your procedure.[105]

Below is yet another sample paragraph and imagined conversation between you and a colleague. Again, remember that you are reading the paragraph while keeping in mind how a well-structured paragraph is written.

Example #2.

> Oppenheimer was so shaken by this personal attack on his behaviors and motives that he did not perform well as a witness on his own behalf. He was evasive and occasionally contradicted himself. His lackluster performance fueled those critics who believed he had been indiscreet – if not frankly disloyal – during the war, and that he had ill-advisedly opposed the development of the hydrogen bomb after the war, and that he failed to cooperate as a witness in the earlier inquiries about his friends and family members. Those attuned to the troubled times and inquisitorial tone of the hearing were not surprised when, on June 28, 1954, the Atomic Energy Commission formally withdrew his security clearance.[106]

---

105 Take a moment to review the example above. Write down the steps to find the main idea of a paragraph. Read the example below and use your steps to see if they work.

106 Gardner, Howard (1995) *Leading Minds: An anatomy of leadership.* Basic Books, New York, p. 104.

After your reading of the paragraph your colleague describes watching you find its main idea:

> The first thing I saw you do was find the topic sentence. You know that the first sentence is usually the topic sentence so you read that sentence carefully. "Oppenheimer was so shaken by this personal attack on his behaviors and motives that he did not perform well as a witness on his own behalf."
>
> The next thing I saw you do was identify the text structure so that you could look for details that supported this topic sentence. The text structure was proposition and support. Sure enough you then found examples of the attacks and how Oppenheimer had hurt himself. Then you determined the main idea of the paragraph and restated it in your own words, "Oppenheimer was judged even more harshly because he did not help his own cause."

Can you now list the steps to finding the main idea in a paragraph?

Step 1: Find topic sentences.

Step 2: Identify text structure.

Step 3: Do following details support the topic sentence?

Step 4: Restate topic sentence.[107]

IMPORTANT: CHECK YOUR STEPS

After you have designed your algorithm, be sure to check it by using the steps to solve the practice problems in any assignment which the students will be assigned.[108] If your steps do not work for all the problems, there are two options. First, you can check to see if all the problems match what you taught. If all the problems do not match, then do not assign them.[109]

---

107 Did you use the same steps?

108 Be careful when you are using published problem sets. Publishers of most adopted texts have not read this book. Many texts will contain problems that vary greatly from the listed objective.

109 Remember the learning progression: Inflexible – Flexible – Application. Most problems in a text will not match a lesson because they do not follow that progression.

Choose only those problems that match. Remember: you are the boss of the book. The book is not the boss of you. Second, you can adjust the steps to make them more generalizable to a greater number of problems.[110] Let's look at a couple examples of this concept of generalizing steps.

Math example #1. Let's use our previous sample math lesson again. As a reminder, the objective for this lesson is to subtract a one-digit number from a two-digit number using regrouping. Even though regrouping during subtraction is the new skill, that does not mean students should regroup while solving every subtraction problem. In fact, having students perform a set of subtraction problems in which regrouping is required in all problems robs students of the opportunity to practice the conditional knowledge required in this skill.

To write a procedure that will work beyond this lesson step 2 could be slightly changed from regroup to *regroup if necessary.*

Step 1: Analyze – which asks the students to determine (1) the type of problem (which operation), and (2) is regrouping necessary?

Step 2: Regroup if necessary – as determined in Step 1.

Although it may seem like a minor distinction, there is a huge difference between a procedure that states 'Regroup' and one that states, 'Regroup if necessary.' A student must be much more cognitively engaged in solving each problem because it is not necessary to regroup in every instance, yet the steps will work in both instances. On the other hand, if students are simply directed in a step to 'Regroup' there will be many struggling students who will regroup even when it is not necessary.

Math example #2. When students initially learn that fractions can be expressed in different ways such as decimal fractions (.7) or as a common fraction with a numerator and denominator (7/10), practice problems may require fractions be converted from one form to another.

It is very common for student texts to sequence learning in such a way that problem sets will have students convert common fractions to decimal fractions in every problem. A sample problem set like this would be:

---

110 This is an example of how to move from inflexible to flexible.

¾ + .30 =

.65 - ⅛ =

½ + .21 =

It would be very tempting for a teacher to write a procedure that directs students to convert the common fraction to a decimal fraction (or vice versa). For example:

Step 1: Analyze - fractions in the same form?

Step 2: Convert common fraction to decimal fraction.

Step 3: Solve.

For the problem set the above procedure would work. But there may be instances in the future where it would make more sense to convert the decimal fraction to a common fraction. Having steps that specify which fraction to convert may work today with this problem set, but they will not work when the conditions change.

An important component of the lesson should be determining which fraction should be converted. Or, stated differently: 'when' should fractions be changed to another form? This is the conditional knowledge that would have been, should have been, taught in the key ideas portion of the lesson. Better, more resilient steps, that would work under various conditions might be:

Step 1: Analyze – fractions same form?

Step 2: Convert if necessary.

Step 3: Solve.

These steps are more generalizable, and they force students to apply *conceptual knowledge* from the lesson.[111] In which situation, and under which conditions, would it be better to convert the common versus the decimal fraction? Determining which fraction to convert would have been part of the key ideas in the lesson.

---

111 Note that these mirror the steps that students will be using when solving early algebra problems, when they must first simplify by combining like terms. Further, these steps will also work if the fractions are representing different units, e.g. 6 inches + ¾ centimeters.

It is always preferable to have more generalizable steps! More generalizable steps force students to analyze problems and conditions and eliminate the need to continuously alter steps.

TIPS FOR DESIGNING PROCEDURES

Tip #1. Keep the steps brief

Most teachers, when they first begin to write procedures for students, provide way too much information. The steps read like a review of the concept and rationale for each step. Well written steps are not meant to be explanations. They are meant simply to be cues.

Cues are sufficient because students will have just observed the teacher model two examples by voicing explanations while solving them.[112] Also, an example problem should remain visible for students as a reminder of what the completed steps look like.

Let's return to the math example above. The listed steps are:

$$\text{Sample problem -} \quad \begin{array}{r} 13 \\ -\ 6 \\ \hline \end{array}$$

Step 1: Analyze – sufficient number of ones to subtract?

Step 2: Regroup – if necessary.

Step 3: Subtract.

Step 4: Answer reasonable?

To further clarify the distinction between explanations, cues, and steps: an explanation is something that the teacher would have *said* during the modeling but would not remain as a visible artifact. An explanation is what students would relate to the teacher during guided practice when retelling what they had done while performing the steps.[113] A cue is merely a few words to help students remember what was modeled.

---

112 The next section on delivery will explain why *two* models.

113 See chapter 7.

| Table 1. Cues vs. Explanation | |
Steps as Cues (Sufficient)	Steps as Explanation (Unnecessary)
Step 1 Analyze (Are there sufficient number of ones to subtract?)	Analyze the problem. "Remember, ask yourself, 'is the number on the bottom bigger than the one on the top?' If it is, then you must regroup."
Step 2 Regroup (if necessary)	If the number on top is bigger, then you don't have to regroup.
Step 3 Subtract	Subtract the Ones. We always start subtracting the numbers on the right. Then subtract the tens.
Step 4 Answer reasonable?	This is a subtraction problem. Is the answer less than the original number?

Tip #2. Steps do not need to be grammatically perfect

Many teachers feel the need to wordsmith the steps of a procedure until the wording is just right. No, beyond just right. Many teachers want the wording to be perfect. They fear if the wording is not just perfect the students will become confused. At this point you have already taught the concept, checked for understanding, and will have modelled two example problems. One of them should be left on the board for students to review as they work through problems using the steps. The example(s) on the board serve as the anchor that students can reference during guided practice.

When I train teachers, I never know what technology or board space will be available. Because of that I bring pre-made posters that I can hang on a wall which have the procedure steps written on it. I use the same posters for multiple training sessions. There have been times, when after a few repetitions using the same steps, I decide there is a better way to express a particular step. I don't create a new poster. I just start using different verbiage. If the teachers in the training have ever noticed that I am saying something slightly different than the way it is written on the poster then they have kept quiet about it. My guess is that they have never even noticed.[114]

---

114 Modeling is so powerful it overpowers written cues.

Tip #3. The procedure must work for all problem types in the lesson

This admonition applies to not only the variation you teach today, but all variations students will encounter around a similar concept. Steps should be general enough to be applicable to variations of the same concept. For example, in order to add fractions, denominators of all addends must be the same. But, the most common sequence for teaching adding fractions is to first teach adding two fractions that have like denominators. Steps for problems that have the same denominator might be written as:

Step 1: Analyze. Same denominators?

Step 2: Add numerators.

Step 3: Sum over denominator.

The next variation might be adding two fractions with unlike denominators.

On the first day it would be tempting to have steps above that do not address the denominators at all. More generalizable steps might be:[115]

Step 1: Analyze. Same denominators?

Step 2: Rewrite with same denominator.

Step 3: Add numerators.

Step:4: Sum over denominator.

By using more generalizable steps students are much more cognitively engaged and are led to employ key ideas presented in the prior lesson component.

Tip #4. Modeled problems should exactly match guided/ independent practice

The problems that are modeled should not be selected randomly. Do not leave anything to chance. Modeled problems should exactly match the type of problems students will be given during guided practice. Similarly, the guided practice problems should exactly match the independent practice problems. By having problems match throughout the lesson formative

---

115 These steps not only work for adding fractions with unlike denominators, they also work for subtraction of fractions.

assessment data collected during the lesson will be predictive of students' performance during independent practice.

If different types of problems are used throughout the lesson and children are not successful it could be indicative of a couple of things. First, the students may not have had enough practice on the problems that most matched the learning objective. Second, as stated early in this book, the teacher may be attempting to teach too much. Indeed, the fact that the problem could be indicative of more than one thing is in itself problematic. Teaching one thing at a time, controlling variables during a lesson, and remaining focused, is what allows students to learn more efficiently. This is also what allows teachers to effectively use formative data to provide instructive and constructive feedback.

Tip #5. Select problems that demonstrate concepts, but with less difficult constituent skills

Even though the teacher is solving the problem, they must still be mindful about problems that might overwhelm students. Students with math phobias can shut down just looking at a problem – for example, if the students recognize bad guys such as 6s, 7s, 8s, fractions, and negative integers.

I once had a discussion with an Algebra teacher regarding her choice of problems while teaching two step equations. Students were fine with the concept of two step equations when coefficients were integers. However, when she used coefficients that were fractions many students were no longer able to solve the equations. I suggested that the problems looked too different to the students. She argued that the process for solving the equations were the same.

Of course the process is the same. Just as walking ten feet across a 12-inch-wide board placed on the floor is the same process as walking ten feet across a 12-inch-wide board that is placed 100 feet off the ground.

To the Algebra teacher, who was proficient with manipulating fractions, the process was the same and looked the same. The problem was she was teaching the lesson to students who were not proficient manipulating fractions. Most students had a fraction phobia so bad that they were freaked out to the point of paralysis when they saw fractions as coefficients.

For the students it was like looking 100 feet down from that 12-inch-wide board.

My point is that from the point of view of students who were not facile in using the inverse of the coefficients to isolate the variable, the equation looked different.

What is the solution? Should the teacher just skip problems that include fractions? Of course not. Just don't do them on the same day the students are learning a new concept. Instead, teach a review lesson, with sufficient practice isolating variables that have fractions as coefficients. Just isolate variables. Don't solve equations. Just isolate variables by using multiplicative inverse of fractions to create coefficients that equal one.[116]

Tip #6. Vary values used in examples
Students attempt to make sense of concepts and skills by looking for patterns. If you model two problems that have the same factors of 4 and 5, and then during guided practice you have the students do problems with the factors of 4 and 5 – even though the problems may yield different results – then there will be students who will think that the new skill or concept only works when the factors are 4 and 5. Mix it up.

DELIVERY TIPS

Tip #1. Model two problems or examples
Always model two example problems. Do not model only one problem because you think the lesson is easy. Do not model three, four or more because you think it is difficult. If two examples are modeled properly, students will be ready to practice. Modeling properly means:

- Having procedure (steps) written on the board.
- Leaving a worked example on the board in close proximity to the steps, or concept maps that students can use as a reference.
- Using Whole – Part – Whole presentation.

---

116 With fraction phobia at epidemic levels, practice with fractions should be occurring nearly daily until students become inoculated.

Why two? We all learn by making patterns. Two points are necessary to define a line. At least two examples are necessary for students to begin to discern a pattern.

For higher performing students, after the first modeled example, the students will hypothesize (silently in their heads) about how the teacher completed the example. The second model confirms or does not confirm the students' hypotheses. For lower performing students, the first model will generate questions. The second model will either answer those questions or make the questions more clear. Teachers have argued that they need to model more because there are several different types of problems in the practice set of problems provided by the textbook. I can almost feel my ears burning. By now most of you know the answer to that argument. Only teach one variation at a time. You are the boss of the book, the book is not the boss of you!

Tip #2. Be the movie

A teacher was about to model. Before she began she asked her 4th grade students, 'When you go to a theater to watch a movie are you supposed to talk while the movie is being played?' The students, of course, answered, 'No.' The teacher then said, 'Well right now I am the movie. While I am modeling these problems all I want you to do is sit and watch me. No questions. No talking.'

Do not allow students to interrupt, question, or contribute during the modeling.[117] In order for the two models to be effective, the students need to see fluent, clean, and clear models. If students are allowed to ask questions some bad things will happen – usually extemporaneous superfluous details.

Bad thing #1. Students are deprived of seeing a clean fluent model (i.e. the 'whole'). When students become involved during the model they seize control from the teacher. Instead of a clean fluent model, the model becomes messy and incoherent.

---

117 I know this goes against the whole 21st century classroom thing about wanting student input, talking to your classmates, etc. In this entire book this is the only time it is recommended to tell students in your nicest teacher voice, 'Shut up and listen'. If you follow this instruction the result will be approximately two minutes when students are not talking, and 38 minutes when they are communicating at a much higher level because of what they have learned.

While I was observing an algebra lesson for a very high performing 7th grade class the teacher began to model. After completing only one step of the procedure a student raised his hand. The student asked a very good and insightful question. The teacher interrupted his model to answer the student's question. As the teacher was done answering the question, a second student raised his hand and asked another very good question. The teacher answered in a very complete and thoughtful manner. When he was done the first student had another good question to which the teacher responded. It was now twenty minutes into the class and the teacher had not yet modeled a single example problem! Teach the class that modeling time is not to be violated. Teach the class that all questions will be answered later.

Bad thing #2. The time it takes to model two problems moves beyond the students' ability to attend. No attention means wasted time.

Two of the easiest ways to become more efficient and complete the key ideas and expert thinking during OWL 1, are to incorporate the above two delivery tips.

Tip #3. Speak in first person
You are the expert. You are explaining how you do the procedure, 'When I see a problem like this the first thing I do is analyze it. Because it is subtraction, I have to ask myself, 'Do I need to regroup?' Students internalize, and memorize, such first person phrasing. As the students begin to practice their internal dialogue will be, 'When I see a problem like this ...'.

Tip #4. Don't be too cute
Think like an expert, not a novice. When solving math problems that include calculation, verbalize that you know how to do the calculation. For example, if one of the steps in the calculation involves multiplying 6×8 just say, 'Six times eight is 48.' Many teachers will attempt to begin to speak as a non-expert and verbalize that calculation like this, 'Well, I have to multiply six time eight. That is a hard one! Let's see: 2 times 8 is sixteen; plus 8 is 24; if 3 times 8 is 24, then six times eight will be 24 plus 24. Let me write that out. Twenty-four plus twenty-four is 48.'

Although the teachers' intentions are good (to model different ways to calculate 6 × 8), it is a waste of time during the lesson. For the students who already know their math facts it is a waste of time. For the students who do not know their math facts it is also a waste of time because just hearing something one more time, without practice, will not make those students better.

FREQUENTLY ASKED QUESTIONS

Q: Can you please explain how to model two problems using Whole – Part – Whole in a procedural lesson?

A: You tell the students, 'Watch me do this problem.' While modeling the first problem you do so from beginning to end. This allows the students to observe the Whole process.

While doing the problem you use teacher talk, speaking in first person, telling students what you are doing. You don't need to explain 'why' – you already covered that during key ideas. What you are doing is using the steps without reading them or drawing attention to them. You complete the problem fluently and without interruption. This is the 'whole'.

After completing the first example you tell the students, 'Let me tell you how I used the steps to solve this problem.' Then retrospectively you point out and read each step while showing the students where that step is reflected in the completed problem. This is the 'part'.

Then you do the second problem telling the students, 'Watch me do another problem. Watch how I use the steps.' Again, you use teacher talk that looks and sounds very much like the first example problem; fluently and without interruption. The difference is this time, you read the step first, and then perform the step. This is the 'whole'.

Q: I teach Kindergarten. Do I still need to write steps and keep them visible even if my students cannot read?

A: Yes, you still need to provide visible steps.

I have seen teachers address students' lack of reading ability in various ways. You can use icons or other symbols instead of words. For example, instead of writing the word 'analyze' some teachers have used a picture of a brain, other teachers have used a pair of eyes, or in the case of language arts lessons the icon may even be a set of ears.

Other teachers use one- or two-word steps. After addressing the steps during modeling using the Whole – Part – Whole structure students begin to become familiar with the words used in the steps. I have witnessed many kindergarten lessons in which students will refer to the steps even if they cannot read them. It is very cute to see students look up to 'read' the steps. Looking at the steps the teacher used helps students to remember what the teacher said and did.

As the year progresses and the reading ability of the students increases, there may be a shift from icons to more written steps.

Q: What do I do if a student has a question while I am modeling?

A: If a student raises their hand during the model, ignore them or quietly motion for them to put their hand down. Do not take time to lecture the class on no questions during modeling. If you do that, you are the one responsible for interrupting the fluent model.

Hopefully this will not happen because you will have reminded your class, 'I am the movie. No hands. No questions.' If a student has a question after the first model, respond by saying, 'Watch me do one more example. If your question isn't answered after the second example, then raise your hand again and I will answer your question then.'

Most questions will be answered during the second model.

Q: What if a student has another method to solve the problem and wants to use his method?

A: If a student has another method to solve the problem, tell them, 'It's great that you know another way! But right now, I want you to do it this way because you are going to need to do it this way when you do tomorrow's lesson.' Or, 'It's great that you know another way, but this is the way we'll solve this problem today.'

Q: What if a group of students look like they 'got it' after a single model?

A: If a student, or group of students, say they get it after the first modeled problem, tell them, 'Great! Watch me do another one and then tell me if I did it the way you thought I would.'

Q: You haven't mentioned taking notes. When do students take notes?

A: NO NOTES during modeling! The amount of time a student can attend is very limited. It just takes too much time for students to take notes. While students are writing the clock is running. Tick tock, tick tock.[118]

When a student is taking notes she is not paying attention to the teacher. There is no such thing as multitasking. At best students are serially tasking, e.g. listening to the teacher, writing notes, listening to the teacher. In the worst case (i.e. the usual case), students are copying notes and not paying attention to the teacher.

At the end of the lesson, after closure, students can take any notes that may seem appropriate. Any information that you as the teacher think should be in a student's notes will be on the board, i.e. sample problems, procedures, etc. Taking notes at this time is more meaningful, and more efficient than copying earlier. Students now know the content and know what is important.

DECLARATIVE LESSONS

In declarative lessons the key ideas and expert thinking components of the lesson morph into an indistinguishable seamless, cohesive explanation of concepts and how to organize those concepts. Much of the information below was included in key ideas. The information provided in key ideas is extended and expanded when the lesson is declarative.

What to model: Students need see information organized

There is so much information available at students' fingertips, why is modeling so important? Why not just point students towards websites,

---

118 Most students, even in the highest achieving classes, usually copy notes. However, copying is a very low level cognitive skill that students will have mastered early in the primary grades.

videos, primary sources, or heaven forbid, a textbook? Students are lacking two important things that prevent the elimination of teachers and students going straight to other sources to become geniuses. Students need basic information about concepts, and they need a structure to help organize the information.

There have been many studies of students' ability to read and comprehend informational text (including audio and visual media). The main determinant of students' ability to successfully comprehend text is their background knowledge. It does not matter how extensive their vocabulary is. It does not matter what their IQ is. If they have never seen a baseball game, they will not be able to comprehend a book about baseball strategy.

Have you ever attempted to teach students to read a text with care? You may have told students to highlight important details as they read. What did the students do? They created a sea of yellow ... because without knowing the content, they had to make the assumption that everything was important. If everything is important, then nothing is important. If a student does not know the content, she will not know what is important.

During expert thinking, the teacher, as the expert, will provide enough background information to the students to allow them to begin cull the unimportant from the important. The teacher does this by telling the story of the concept through presenting students with an overview.

Even with an overview of the information, as novices the students still need the teacher to model how she organizes the information. Without organization information can be overwhelming. The teacher is modeling when she explains how she uses the organizational structure to understand information about the concept. This is her expert thinking.

Telling the story and providing an organizational structure was also discussed in the previous chapter on key ideas. Teachers tell the story, they provide an organizational structure using a concept map, and they provide a language frame that supports students' articulation of the concepts.

How to model: Whole – Part – Whole
When modeling during declarative lessons teachers use the Whole – Part – Whole delivery structure. This structure was discussed earlier in this

chapter with respect to modeling a procedure. Whatever we are learning, the Whole – Part – Whole structure makes that learning easier.

Let's start with the 'whole' – teachers tell the story of the concept they are teaching. The story, as described earlier, is a brief overview of the concept.[119] When I describe the story to teachers, I tell them to think of the initial part of a *Wikipedia* entry. There is always a concise overview of the topic in just a few paragraphs or lines. That is the story.

Let's return to the poverty lesson first introduced in chapter 5.[120] Here is the 'whole' the teacher would present to students. It is an overview of the concept of generational poverty, the background knowledge. It is the story.

> In economics, a **poverty trap** or **cycle of poverty** is caused by self-reinforcing mechanisms that cause poverty. Once it exists, it will continue unless there is outside intervention, and can persist across generations. Families trapped in the cycle of poverty, have either limited or no resources. There are many disadvantages that collectively work in a circular process making it virtually impossible for individuals to break this cycle, such as lack of access to financial capital, education, or social connections. In other words, impoverished individuals often do not posess the economic and social resources required to escape their poverty. This could mean that the poor remain poor throughout their lives.

A concept map is a visual representation of the story. Choose the concept map that best represents the story told.[121] In this case (the cycle of poverty) the concept map that depicts a cycle is the obvious choice. Is it really always that easy to choose a concept map? With practice, yes, it is.

---

119 See chapter 7.

120 Learning objective: students will write an essay describing a family in a poverty trap using the concept of the cycle of poverty.

121 The only six maps you will need to choose from are in appendix I.

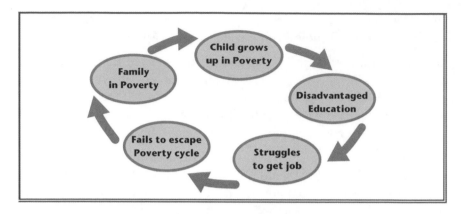

Because the story is an overview, a big picture, there are only a few details included. These details will populate the concept map, they are the parts. The concept map provides a visual form for the 'part' component of the Whole – Part – Whole structure. In this example, the details of the poverty cycle are: A child grows up in poverty. They have a disadvantaged education. Because of poor education, they struggle to get a good job. Without a good job the family stays in poverty. The cycle returns to the child in poverty.

At this point in the lesson the teacher would provide students with a vignette that describes a family suffering multigenerational poverty. The teacher would model how specific details in the vignette match the general organization of information presented in the concept map. In this example the teacher would model two examples of locating where a person or family in poverty is in the poverty cycle trap using the concept map to help her understand the person's or family's poverty. The teacher models the two examples using the language frame (while pointing to the cycle concept map).

Language frame

I know this person is receiving a <u>sub-par education</u>. Without a good education it will be <u>difficult for this person to get a good job</u>. Without a good job it will be difficult to <u>escape poverty</u>.

The teacher models how she uses the organizational structure to understand new information. The teacher models how the cycle concept map helps her understand new content about generational poverty. This modelling is the second 'whole' in the Whole – Part – Whole process.

Someone observing a declarative lesson but not familiar with the FAST Framework might not be able to discern when key ideas morph into modeling. In declarative lessons there is not a clear, distinct, discrete line between key ideas and expert thinking. This is because in both components teachers rely on concept maps and language frames (the latter are linguistic representations of the concept maps).

The simplest way to think about this morphing is that during key ideas the teacher lays out the general structure of the concept. During key ideas the definitions are clear and straightforward. For example – referring back to the poverty example above – if a family has one or more of the listed characteristics, they are in poverty. That is the presentation of key ideas. It is clear and unambiguous.[122] During modeling the teacher models how information from another context fits into the general framework.

DESIGN TIPS FOR DECLARATIVE LESSONS

Tip #1. Choose the two examples you will model with care
You want the examples to work exactly with the concept map and language frame. It is not the time to see how much you can stretch the students' thinking about a new concept. Remember! Inflexible first, then flexible, and finally application.

Tip #2. During initial lessons in a unit change the context but stay concrete
Complex concepts are derived from more simple concepts that seem to evolve. Break the complex into more manageable tasks that when stacked upon each other make learning doable for students. Remember, the number one reason students are not successful is that teachers are attempting to teach too much.

In the poverty lesson above, the ultimate goal is to *eventually* study generational poverty to analyze legislation meant to address the issue. How many declarative lessons will it take to get all the students to that place? Maybe three. Maybe four. The point is to go slow to go fast. Some

---

122 See appendix II.

teachers believe this is dumbing down the content. To the contrary, presenting concepts in increasing levels of complexity allows many more students to be successful with increasingly sophisticated content.

Here is an example illustrating the natural desire of teachers to accelerate instruction to more complex information before students are ready. While training teachers in the FAST Framework, I always present a model lesson in which the teachers assume the role of students. The content is always part of a state standard, but also something that is sophisticated enough that the teachers will never have learned it well, or it is something they have forgotten. During one particular training session the attendees were teacher-leaders on campus. All the disciplines were represented. The learning objective for the lesson was: students will analyze events to determine if they are a constitutional crisis.

After the lesson teachers had the opportunity to give feedback on the lesson. The lesson, as a teaching tool, had been successful in that the teachers were able to discern how the lesson components flowed together. The lesson was also successful because teachers met the learning objective and they learned about constitutional crises.

The only negative comment regarding the lesson was from a very well-respected teacher from the social studies department. 'The lesson was okay as far as it went, but a constitutional crisis is much more complicated than how it was presented,' he said. My reply was, 'Of course it is! It is much, much, more complicated. But it is not complicated in today's lesson.'

My point is that almost anything worth learning is complex. The teacher's role is to make the complex learnable through a series of more simple lessons.[123] The cumulative effect will be complex.

Inflexible Knowledge - Flexible Knowledge - Application.

Tip #3. Select a concept map you will be using in the lesson

What type of concept map should be used? Not to be too repetetive, but the name of this component is 'expert thinking'. How do you think about the concept? Proposition and support? Cause and effect? Choose the map that matches your thinking.

---

123 See chapter 5.

There are multiple ways to think about most topics. Several teachers in a high school social studies department once shared how they thought about World War II.

The first teacher said, 'I think about WWII chronologically' (i.e. a sequence map).

The next teacher said, 'I think about it with respect to the different theaters - Pacific, Europe, and Africa' (i.e. a tree map).

The last teacher said, 'I think about it in terms of the impact of major battles' (i.e. a cause and effect map).

Which is correct? All of them are correct. Don't overthink it. Listen to yourself as you explain a concept and the concept map and the corresponding language frame will present itself.

Tip #4: Construct a language frame that matches the concept map

Have you ever had a student say, 'I know what it is, I just can't explain it.' The language frame focuses the germane cognitive load on the new concept while reducing extraneous load.

Tip #5. Students must already possess the skills necessary to complete any task designated as the learning objective or independent practice!

If the students will be asked to write an essay on a topic, they should already know how to write an essay. A teacher does not have time to teach a skill – like how to write an essay – at the same time she is teaching other content.[124] This admonition does not discount the utility of presenting a completed example to the students. 'This is an example of a good essay,' or 'This is a rubric for the essay,' is very different from modeling how to write an essay.

If students do not currently possess the skills to develop a well written essay, then the teacher needs to change the learning objective. Writing an essay is not the only way to demonstrate knowledge of a concept. Students could complete an organizer, make a list, create slides, identify

---

124 Note the chart in appendix IV. In declarative lessons the skill is *never* new.

and describe, etc. There are many ways for students who cannot yet write an essay to demonstrate new knowledge.[125]

DELIVERY TIPS IN A DECLARATIVE LESSON

Tip #1. Model only two examples on the concept map

During modeling, examples presented should be straight forward and exactly match the concept map. Using the poverty example, and the corresponding cycle concept map (see p. 128), the teacher could choose two examples of people or families in the cycle of generational poverty.

Cite two examples of the new key idea(s) and how the new concept relates to pre-instruction thinking or prior knowledge. The citation of two examples may exist in a single piece of text. The text being used may include many more examples, but you only need to model two.

Tip #2. Refer back to the concept map during Q and A, discussions, etc.

Show how what is being discussed relates to the main concepts.

Tip #3. Use the language frames

Demand the students use the language frames. Using language frames reduces extraneous cognitive load and frees more brain power for understanding the concept.

If a student asks, 'Can I answer in my own words?'

Respond with, 'Sure you can answer in your own words. But use the language frame first.'

ANOTHER LESSON EXAMPLE: USING SENSORY DETAILS

Imagine a lesson with the following learning objective: 'students will identify uses of sensory details in poetry.' What type of concept map might

---

125 This is not to say a teacher should not have a long-term goal of teaching students how to write a well-developed essay. It means that the teacher should not confuse a lesson on generational poverty with a writing lesson. This is a good example of why it is important to collaborate with teachers in other disciplines.

you use for this lesson? My guess is a tree map with five boxes, each listing one of the senses and giving a few examples of sensory words.

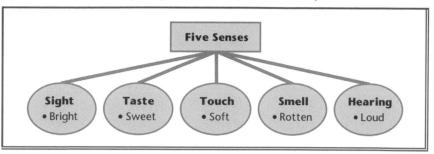

Language frame

I know the word _____ is a sensory detail because it makes me think of something I can _____.

It is possible in this example that two sensory details may appear in a single stanza of a poem or even in the first few lines of a poem. If this is the case, the teacher will be able to model both examples in those few lines.

Lets consider the poem 'White' by Maggie Mendoza, one of a number of color poems using sensory details which she has developed as classroom resources.

White is a cool breeze,

Wind on my cheek,

A whisper.

Sandwiches at lunch,

Wholesome milk,

Soft, puffy marshmallows in hot chocolate.

My younger sister's laughter

Echoing down the hall.

Lacey angel wings

Mounds of snow and snowball fights.

Clouds drifting across the sky on this

Beautiful morning.[126]

After the teacher has presented a tree map that has the five senses and examples of sensory details to the students, she will begin to reread the poem.[127] The teacher stops after she comes to a sensory detail.

'When I read the words, "White is a cool breeze," I imagine feeling cool. When I look at my tree map of the senses I see that the sense of touch is feeling. So I would say "cool" is a sensory detail.' The teacher then uses the language frame:

> I know the phrase <u>"White is cool breeze"</u> is a sensory detail because it makes me think of something I can <u>feel</u>.

The teacher selects another line in the poem. It does not have to be the next line. It should be an example that is clear to the children. 'When I read the line, "Echoing down the hall", I know that an echo is a sound. When I look at my tree map of the senses, I see that hearing is about sounds. So, I would say that "echoing" is sensory detail.' The teacher then uses the language frame:

> I know the word <u>"echoing"</u> is a sensory detail because it makes me think of something I can <u>hear</u>.

'Are there any questions? Great! Now it is your turn.'

The modeling began when the concept of sensory details moved from a definition to an application of the definition in a different context.

At this point the teacher has modeled twice. Many teachers have confused modeling two *examples* with having to model two *poems*. There are more than ten instances of sensory imagery in this poem. You only need to model two examples, or instances, of the use of sensory details, not two poems. If the teacher were to model identifying all the sensory details in just this simple poem, there would be no time left for the students to practice.

---

126 'White' along with other color poems using sensory details and indeed numerous other classroom resources across language arts, writing, math and other subjects are available from https://www.teacherspayteachers.com/Store/Maggie-Meadows.

127 This poem would probably previously have been read as part of the preview.

Approximate time to complete:
5-12 minutes

Depending on age of students

COMPONENT CONNECTIONS

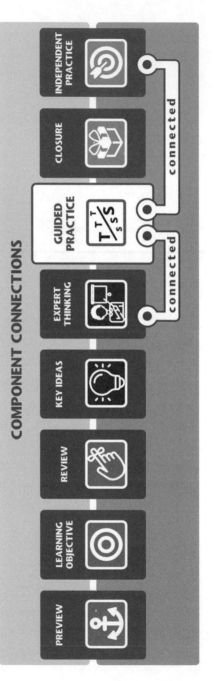

PREVIEW

LEARNING OBJECTIVE

REVIEW

KEY IDEAS

EXPERT THINKING

GUIDED PRACTICE

CLOSURE

INDEPENDENT PRACTICE

connected

connected

CHAPTER 7
GUIDED PRACTICE

Big ideas in guided practice:

- Guided practice is the second of the two biggest time savers.
- Students learn by practicing.
- Practice is designed to reinforce both concepts and skills.
- Guided practice has two goals: practice for the students, data for the teacher.
- Students are immediately 100% responsible for practicing new skills and concepts.

There are three big timesavers in this chapter:

1. Limit the number of guided practice questions to three.
2. Limit the amount of time allowed to students to complete each step.
3. Limit feedback to the entire class.

These changes can reduce the amount of time typically spent on guided practice by more than 50%. As with the two prior chapters on key ideas and expert thinking, guided practice for procedural lessons and declarative lessons will be addressed in separate sections.

OVERVIEW

Have you ever wanted to learn how to play golf or speak a new language? You may have read a book or watched videos in an attempt to teach yourself. Even though you watched the videos and practiced faithfully, you were unsure if your swing was quite right. You were unsure if your pronunciation of a particular word was correct. You had no way of knowing if you were practicing correctly or if you were wasting your time. Eventually, you became frustrated with your progress and decided to take some lessons from a qualified teacher. Or, at the very least, you recruited a knowledgeable friend to give you some feedback. In no time, after some instructive and constructive feedback, you corrected your mistakes and began to make great progress.

It is the very rare learner who becomes competent in a new concept or skill by simply watching or listening to someone talk. We learn when we actually engage in the task and receive feedback. We learn when we begin to practice.

Effective guided practice immediately provides students with both practice and feedback. In procedural lessons students are required to engage immediately in solving problems (or, in the early stages, immediately solving parts of problems). In declarative lessons, the students immediately engage with concepts in various cognitively challenging contexts.[128]

Classroom learning occurs in predictable sequences. The first part of the sequence is the teachers' instruction, which includes explanation of the concepts and modeling of skills. But the lasting learning, the learning that leads to mastery, occurs in the second part of the sequence. Real learning, lasting learning, and mastery is an outcome of effective practice. Effective practice begins under the watchful eye of an expert.

---

128 Many skills have multiple constituent skills that may be too much to teach in a single lesson. Many skills need to be chunked and sequenced over several lessons. In such cases students may not be practicing a complete procedure but parts of it.

Guided practice is the first opportunity in a lesson for students to fully engage with the new content. In order to get to student practice quickly teachers work effectively and efficiently through the previous lesson components.[129] Guided practice is the first opportunity for teachers to formatively assess all students on the new concepts and skills.

Effective guided practice includes both constructive and instructive feedback based upon formative data. When the teacher provides constructive feedback, she informs the student what they did not do correctly. Instructive feedback informs the student how to perform the task correctly.

Constructive and instructive feedback can be either direct, indirect, or a combination of the two. Direct feedback is exactly what it sounds like; the teacher directly informs the student. A teacher using indirect feedback allows students to be self-critical through guided questioning. Providing feedback is part of the science of teaching. How the teacher chooses to provide feedback, direct or indirect, is part of the art of teaching.

Goals for guided practice

There are two goals for guided practice. The first goal is for students; the second goal is for teachers. The goal for students is to begin multiple repetitions of practice, with feedback, as quickly as possible. The goal for teachers is to gather formative data as quickly as possible.

Using formative data collected from a well-designed, well-delivered, and effective guided practice, the teacher can quickly bifurcate the class into groups. One group are those who are ready to continue their practice independently, and the other group are those students who need additional support through a short and highly focused immediate in-class intervention.

Effective guided practice reinforces both concepts and skills

Anders Ericsson, the psychologist who first expressed the 10,000 hours of practice rule (later popularized by Malcolm Gladwell), describes the elements of effective practice in *Peak: Secrets from the new science of*

---

129 This is the students' first opportunity to practice during the lesson. It should occur within 6-16 minutes of the start of the lesson.

expertise (2016).[130] Ericsson says that for practice to be effective students should explain concepts each time they practice an algorithm. *In this way each repetition not only helps students achieve automaticity of the algorithm, but also reinforces the concept behind it.*

As the students begin to practice and engage in the new skill, a broader, deeper conceptual understanding should also result from the practice. Proper design of the algorithm, the procedure, will have embedded the concepts in the procedures that were modeled. For example, let's return to the subtraction with regrouping lesson from previous chapters. Embedded in the regrouping procedure is the important concept that regrouping is the creation of an equivalent number. Ten and four is the same as 14. That is why the regrouping procedure is a valid mathematical procedure. Regrouping has not changed values. This concept should be reinforced during each repetition by the students during guided practice. The students can reinforce the concept as they perform the problem. The teacher may prompt them by saying, 'Tell your partner why it is okay to regroup?'

PROCEDURAL LESSONS

A gradual release of responsibility
Students are 100% responsible for immediately performing new skills. Effective and efficient initial practice occurs when students immediately engage in the new skill following the teacher's modeling.[131] Students must begin to practice immediately *and* independently. Most students are not ready to practice an entire new procedure independently so the procedures should be broken down in such a way as to make the smaller constituent parts achievable immediately.

---

130 Ericsson, A. & Pool, R. (2016) *Peak: Secrets from the new science of expertise.* Houghton Mifflin, New York, NY.

131 There are those in the field of education who advocate for students attempting to practice new skills without teacher modeling. The idea is to let students engage in 'productive struggle' by allowing the students to 'figure it out' for themselves. Two thoughts on this issue: (1) the research is clear that such an approach is effective for only the highest performing students who already bring foundational skills and background knowledge to the lesson, and (2) teachers end up modeling after the students have 'struggled productively' because the students need instruction. Why not just model up front? It does not hurt anyone, but it certainly helps many students.

Guided practice has been accurately described as a gradual release of responsibility.[132] This gradual release of responsibility should be planned and systematic. Students are able to immediately perform parts of the procedure independently because the teacher has modeled them using a step-by-step procedure (see chapter 6).

The gradual release of responsibility is represented on the FAST Framework with the icon T/s T/S t/S. This icon is sometimes misinterpreted to mean that initially the teachers are doing most of the work, and gradually the responsibility for doing the work is transferred to the students. That is both incorrect and ineffective.

The big T does not represent who is doing the work, as stated above, *the students are immediately doing 100% of the work.* The size of the first 'T' represents how much control of the practice process is being exerted by the teacher. Initially (i.e. T/s), maximum control is exerted by the teacher; as practice progresses (i.e. t/S) minimal control is exerted. The release of responsibility is release of *control of the procedure* to the students.

The teacher exerts control of the process through her directions, but it is the students who are doing all, 100%, of the work.[133]

---

132 Gradual release of responsibility is yet another of those terms used by many educators. Do not confuse the gradual release of responsibility described in this chapter with other methodologies sometimes described as GRR. The GRR method is a macro idea i.e. a gradual release across the entire lesson. The gradual release described in this chapter is micro, a gradual release of responsibility during the initial guided practice.

133 This is one of the most important differences in the FAST Framework versus other methods of guided practice or gradual release. It is the difference that makes all the difference.

Designing guided practice: Gradual release

The main design consideration for guided practice is how the gradual release will occur. A gradual release of responsibility is easy to visualize in a procedural lesson where students are initially directed to perform a single step of procedure on their own, then perform multiple steps of the procedure on their own, and finally the entire procedure on their own. This description is accurate and edifying in helping to understand guided practice in a procedural lesson as shown in the example below.

Example #1. After the teacher has modeled two problems she should ask the students if they have any questions. If students have questions that would be answered by performing the task, then the teacher proceeds to the guided practice problems. If students have questions that would not be answered by doing problems, then the teacher has the option of answering the question if it advances the entire class's understanding of the current lesson.[134] However, if answering the question would only satisfy the curiosity of the student asking the question, the teacher should acknowledge the question and in a very polite way say 'Thanks for asking. We will talk about that later', and then continue with the lesson.

Design the gradual release to occur over at least three practice problems. Using the regrouping problem from previous chapters as an example, the gradual release of responsibility would look like this:

Sample problem - $\begin{array}{r} 13 \\ - \ 6 \\ \hline \end{array}$

Step 1: Analyze – are there sufficient number of ones to subtract.

Step 2: Regroup – if necessary.

Step 3: Subtract.

Step 4: Is answer reasonable?

---

134 Many teachers view good questions that are pertinent to the content, but not necessarily related to the current lesson as 'teachable moments.' Teachable moments are not such instances. Such questions are flights of fancy and bird-walking. Good questions should be encouraged and answered – after the lesson. Understanding the time limitations that impact effective instruction helps teachers to make decisions about whether something is worthy of the precious time that exists to teach lessons. Tick tock, tick tock.

The next several pages describe a method of teacher facilitation that will reduce the amount of time spent during guided practice by more than 50%.

During the first guided practice problem, the teacher will direct students to, 'Do step 1 and stop.'[135] After the students perform the step, the teacher checks the students' responses to gather data on how they performed. If most students have the correct answer the teacher then echoes, or remodels, the correct response on the whiteboard. On the other hand, if a number of students answered incorrectly, the teacher would take a moment to re-explain whatever issues were confounding the students after she echoes the correct response.[136] The teacher always adds the admonition, 'If your board does not look like mine, change it now.'[137] This process is another example of using the Whole – Part – Whole approach: show the correct answer, explain how you got that answer, then show the correct answer again.

There does not need to be more than a few students answering incorrectly for the teacher to take a few seconds to remodel that particular step. Remodeling allows the students who did not perform the step correctly to see the step retaught. The new iteration of the explanation is more meaningful because students had tried and were unsuccessful. The students' interaction with the problem provides additional context for the additional explanation. Remodeling is quick and helps those students who

---

135 Throughout the explanation of how to perform guided practice there will be references to the teacher checking students' work. We recommend the use of erasable white boards, sometimes referred to as MWBs. Why? There have been studies that show when students can easily erase, they are more apt to make attempts even when they are unsure. Compare that to students using paper and pencil erasing work, tearing papers and generally making a mess. Also, a teacher can quickly check a class of whiteboards that students are holding in the air, versus having to walk around and check students individually. I have yet to see another technology that match the speed of the whiteboards for certain lessons.

136 If students find a particular step in a procedure problematic, especially after the teacher has re-explained, the teacher may present additional practice, and check for understanding of that problematic step. In the majority of lessons, most times, the practice and checking for understanding just described, would have occurred during key ideas.

137 In this lesson there is a correct response to each step. In many lessons, especially in other subject areas, there is not necessarily a single correct response. In that case, the teacher, after remodeling, may say something like, 'Does anyone have a different response?'

need an additional explanation. Because the teacher is only explaining, or remodeling, one step in the procedure it literally takes seconds. The students evaluate their own work.

What about the students who were successful? Having the students watch the teacher for 30 seconds while she is remodeling does not hurt them one bit. In fact, it is probably ego boosting.[138]

Next, while still on the same first problem, the teacher directs students, 'Do step 2 and stop.' After the teacher has directed the students to perform a particular step SHE MUST STOP TALKING! The inclination of most teachers is to continue to give clues about how to perform the step. We frequently hear, 'Do step 2 and stop. Remember if the bottom number was bigger you are going to have to regroup. If you have to regroup, don't forget to rewrite the number in the 10s.' And on and on. Teachers: Give yourself credit for doing a good job teaching the key ideas and modeling. STOP TALKING!

The teacher then repeats the process checking the students' responses in order to gather data on how they performed on step 2. The teacher then echoes (i.e. remodels), the correct response. If a large majority of the class answered correctly, the teacher will move on. On the other hand, if a number of students answered incorrectly, the teacher would take a moment to re-explain, remodel, as described above, whatever issues were confounding the students.

Next, the teacher instructs 'Do step 3 and stop,' and follows the process above. Finally, the teacher directs, 'Do step 4 and stop,' and repeats the process above.

It is possible that a large number of students were not successful completing each step during the first practice problem. This is not a reason to interrupt the flow of the guided practice. The learning curve is very steep from the first repetition to the second repetition. Remember the students are attempting to incorporate two ideas during the first guided practice. First, students are learning what should happen during each step of the procedure. Second, the students are also learning the new skill.

---

138 The teacher might even add a comment for students who were correct. 'If you had the correct answer, watch while I do it and see if you did it the same way I did.'

IMPORTANT: Please note how the teacher exerted total control of the first practice problem by directing students to perform only a single step of the procedure and then stopping. *Even though the teacher exerted control of the process, the students were immediately doing 100% of the work!*

After the teacher determines and mentally notes which students are not performing well, she proceeds to the next guided practice problem. The teacher's directions and responses are the same as above *except*, now the teacher begins to exert *less control* by gradually releasing more responsibility to the students. The teacher directs the students to do more work by combining steps before checking the students' work. For example, instead of saying, 'Do step 1 and stop'. the directions are, 'Do step 1 and step 2 and stop.'[139]

If students are having difficulty performing a particular constituent skill, the teacher can tell the class, 'I will be doing the problem at the same time. If you are still having a problem with this step, you can look at the board for help.'[140] The only students who will look at the board are those who need help. The other students will do the work on their own.

Just like during the first problem, the teacher checks the students' responses to gather data on how they performed. The teacher then performs steps 1 and 2, echoes the correct response for the class, and remodels those steps. If a large majority of the class answered correctly, the teacher will move on. On the other hand, if a large number of students answered incorrectly, the teacher would take a moment to re-explain whatever issues were confounding the students.

Then the teacher directs, 'Do step 3 and step 4 and stop.' The teacher follows the same routine. When she is satisfied that she has data from everyone, it is time for the final problem. At this point the teacher relinquishes total control to the students. 'This time,' the teacher says, 'do the whole problem by yourself.'

---

139 How long do you think it should take students to determine that is 3 is greater than 7 and to regroup? Less than 30 seconds? Less than 20 seconds? Less than 5 seconds? In most cases students don't need more time; they need more instruction.

140 Remember, a constituent skill is necessary to perform a particular step, e.g. knowing math facts. Learning math facts is not the objective of the lesson.

The teacher has now relinquished total control to the students. The teacher checks the responses to gather data. The teacher follows the same routine of echoing responses and remodeling.

By the end of the third problem, the class will have become bifurcated. The larger group will be the students who are able to move to independent practice. The much smaller group will need immediate in-class intervention.

Occasionally, very infrequently, four guided practice problems are needed. If you, as the teacher, determine an additional guided practice problem is needed, the release should not be like the first problem, in which the teacher stops students at each step. Nor should it be like the final problem in which students perform the entire problem. The combination of steps for the additional problem should be more like the second problem (bridging from that to the final problem). The teacher will combine the steps that the students are able to do and keep separate the steps in which the students need to focus.

Scaffolding steps

Please note that in the example above the teacher directs the students to do step 1 and then she is quiet. In the above example step 1 is 'analyze.' The direction from the teacher is to tell the students, 'Do step 1.'

How can the teacher provide scaffolding for this step while still demanding that the students do 100% of the work? Before directing the students to do step 1 (i.e. analyze), the teacher could direct the students, 'Tell your partner, 'What is step 1?'' Further scaffolding questions might include:

- 'Tell your partner: What are we analyzing?'
- 'Students, put your fingers on the digits we are analyzing.'
- 'Check with your partner to see if you are both pointing at the same digit.'

When designing a lesson it is best to include ways to check for understanding, such as pointing or having students students circle what they are comparing.

Providing student feedback

You may have noticed that in the above description of gradual release the teacher did not take time to correct individual students. All feedback was directed at the entire class. Students are required to check their own work and make appropriate changes. Teachers should not attempt to correct and/or help individual students during the guided practice.[141] Taking time to help individual students during guided practice is not efficient or effective for several reasons:

- It interrupts the pace of the lesson.

- Many times teachers are helping students perform lower level or constituent skills, e.g. helping with math facts.

- If a student truly cannot perform an individual step there is nothing the teacher can do in 30 seconds or a minute that will provide that student with enough assistance to remediate the student's deficit.

Providing immediate, individual help for students is a very difficult habit for most teachers to break. Helping children is why most teachers go into teaching.

Before teachers change their helping routines from providing immediate help to waiting before providing help, they need to explain to students the change in routine. Inform students that help will be provided, just not at this moment. If what seems like ignoring students is not specifically explained, students will feel ignored, disliked, picked upon, etc.

Students need to be taught that if they cannot perform a step, and the teacher is not going to provide immediate one-to-one support, it does not mean they are off the hook during guided practice. In fact, they have even more responsibility. They may not be able to perform a particular step, but they are still responsible for copying the step as the teacher remodels.[142] The FAST Framework is a very high accountability model for students.

---

141 The exception to this 'do not help' rule is if you, the teacher, can give a 2-3 second cue while walking past a student such as, 'check you addition,' or 'check your signs.' This type of feedback can get students back on track without taking time and attention from the entire class.

142 Remember when the teacher said in the above example, 'If your board doesn't look like mine, change it.'

Of course, you will help them. Just not now. This is not about productive struggle.[143] This is about understanding the structure of the FAST Framework and how it matches how students learn.

Changing when you provide help to students (so that it is after guided practice), is beneficial to the students who are struggling because you can give them your full attention. It is also beneficial to the students who are not struggling as they will be allowed to work at a faster pace because the teacher has not slowed down the lesson. Tick tock, tick tock.

DESIGN TIPS

Tip #1. Estimate how long each step should take
After planning the procedure ask yourself, 'How long should it take the students to perform this step?' For example, how long should it take students in step 1 to determine if 6 is greater than 3? 3 seconds? 5 seconds? If you think it should take 5 seconds, then give them 8 seconds. If a student cannot determine that 6 is greater than 3 in eight seconds, he doesn't need more time, he needs more instruction.

Tip #2. Plan ahead for how to combine steps
The first repetition should always be one step at a time. The final repetition should always be the students doing all the steps. The middle repetition(s) – the one(s) in which steps are combined – should be thoughtfully planned. When combining steps, ask yourself, 'Which steps naturally flow together?' It is nearly impossible to stop students from progressing to the next step if the next step is literally right there. For example, with the math problem above, once the students have regrouped it would be nearly impossible to stop them from subtracting.

---

143 'Productive struggle' may be the most abused buzz-words in education today. Problem solving as a way to learn is misunderstood. Learning a standard algorithm is not problem solving. Teaching students constituent skills involved in solving a problem does not have to be difficult for students. We shouldn't be asking students to figure out some algorithm when it can be taught and practiced in a single class period. Solving problems involves the *application of skills as they relate to the real world, or hypothetical situations.*

Tip #3. Determine how to check each step

One of the reasons using steps is so efficient and effective is that teachers can collect discrete data on every student's progress. Data can only be collected when students are asked to do something physically. For example, in the above subtraction example, in step 1 students are asked to analyze. In this problem 'analyze' means the students will compare two numbers. You can't see inside their heads when they compare, but you can ask them to point to the two numbers being compared. You can ask them to say what the two numbers are. Having the students do something physically, e.g. point, verbalize, circle, etc. gives the teacher discrete information (formative data) regarding the students' performance.

DELIVERY TIPS

Tip #1. Stop talking

Once you have directed students to do a particular step or steps, STOP TALKING! Let the students make honest mistakes. In educationese we call that formative data.

Tip #2. Make feedback brief for incorrect responses

Feedback is general and to the entire class. Feedback is also mostly instructive as you are re-modeling the correct answer.

Tip #3. Provide intervention after closure

It bears repeating, there is nothing you can do in a few seconds to remediate most issues that students have during a lesson. When you help an individual student you leave an entire class waiting. Nothing good ever comes from that. Tick tock, tick tock.

FREQUENTLY ASKED QUESTIONS

Q: I know you said that teachers should only model two problems. I am just not convinced that students don't need to see more models before they start practicing. Is it okay to model more problems?

A: During the modeling component the teacher models two problems, two. One of the reasons for only providing two models during expert thinking is to move the students to guided practice as quickly as possible.

In the description of guided practice above, you will notice that the teacher 'remodels'. During guided practice students will see the teacher model a minimum of three more times within the context of new problems.

Q: *What do I do with students who go ahead and do more steps I than directed?*

A: *Gently say, 'Please don't go ahead. Erase everything on your board except Step___ .'*

Q: *I have students who will not want to stop at step 1. Or, when I say, 'Do step 2 and stop.' How do I stop students from going ahead? I already have asked them to stop as you suggested above.*

A: *Try this, 'I know you are excited, and you want to go faster. But when you go ahead it takes me longer to find your answer on your whiteboard. When you go ahead you are actually slowing down the lesson.'*

Q: *Why can't I give needed support to struggling students during guided practice? Why not let the students who 'get' the lesson go ahead? Aren't I hurting them by holding them back?*

A: *In order to help students who are struggling a teacher must diagnose, teach, prescribe, and monitor students' practice. To effectively help students who are struggling in 30 seconds, or 60 seconds, is just not possible. You will feel rushed. The students will feel rushed. You will not be successful.*

And, by the way, what do you think the rest of the class is doing when you are spending your time and attention on single students? You probably don't want to know what the rest of the class is doing …

Regarding the students who 'get' it. There are a couple of responses. First, use the strategy mentioned earlier about determining how long a step will take. Hold the students to that time. Using this strategy, students who 'get it' quickly will not have to wait long. It will only be a matter of seconds. Second, embedded in the guided practice are concepts that should be articulated by students to either a partner or the teacher during each repetition. If students are allowed to go ahead, they will miss the opportunity to recall and relearn that information.

One of the classroom procedures you need to teach your class is how you will respond to questions during guided practice. Your commitment to the students is to get through guided practice as quickly as you can. The students who 'get it' benefit from the class moving quickly because they want to do the work. The students who are struggling benefit from the commitment because the quicker the class can get through guided practice, the sooner they will get help. Tick tock, tick tock.

Students need to know that if they are struggling you will help them. The help will not be immediate, but it is coming. It is important that students know you are not ignoring them. The fact that you will be providing extra help later does not absolve them of the responsibility of making their whiteboards 'look like mine.' Even if students are copying responses that the teacher has remodeled, they are responsible for copying.

Having said that, here is an idea to keep students who finish quickly occupied. Every teacher has 'sponge activities' in their back pockets for those times when there are a few minutes before dismissal or lunch, etc. The sponge activities are designed to keep students occupied but also provide academic benefit. For example, the teacher may call on students to practice math facts, spelling words, or whatever else. If students are able to complete this activity, fine. If students are not able to complete the activity, fine. Whenever the teacher calls time and stops the activity is fine.

During guided practice the idea is to ask students sponge questions or give sponge directions. For example, you direct students to do step 1 and stop. As you walk around you see a couple of students who have completed the step. As you pass them you can whisper, 'Explain to each other what you just did.' It doesn't matter if they finish the explanation or not. They were doing something of quality and not feeling like they were being held back.

NOTES FROM THE FIELD

A very strong 5th grade teacher was telling me how she managed her math class. The teacher had three math groups: high, medium, and low. The groups had cute names to spare students' feelings. But guess what? The students knew what each group represented.

The teacher began each math class with a brief lesson for all students. During this brief lesson, the teacher would present the 'big ideas' of the lesson. There would be no practice.

The class would then be assigned some practice problems while she worked with each of the small groups. Some of the problems were from the prior day's lesson and some problems were from the current lesson. The teacher worked with each small group for ten minutes guiding them through the practice problems.

The teacher, subsequent to training and coaching in the FAST Framework, realized that if the guided practice is performed in the manner described above it was unnecessary to work with each group. The biggest 'aha' the teacher had was that she had been pre-judging how students would perform in any particular lesson.

The teacher continued to pull a group to provide additional assistance, but it was only after all students had the opportunity to demonstrate proficiency during the lesson. She realized that there were many lessons in which the students in the 'low' group did not need additional help. The group that needed immediate intervention was fluid.

Most teachers will proclaim they have high expectations for all their students. Teachers cannot proclaim they have high expectations if they continue to design classroom structures that do not allow students the opportunity to succeed.

If teachers' expectations are that students will not perform today – just as they did not perform yesterday – then the students will meet those low expectations. Teachers must design lessons that provide the best opportunity for students to be successful every day. The FAST Framework provides the structure for well-designed lessons.

DECLARATIVE LESSONS

Analyzing guided practice: An increasing cognitive demand of questions

Reframing what is occurring cognitively during the gradual release in declarative lessons may help understand the process. Daniel T. Willingham states that the progression of learning is from 'inflexible', to 'flexible', then to 'application'.[144] He describes these as necessary phases. During a lesson – and over several lessons – students' thinking moves from, 'What are the basic facts around this information? To, 'How are these facts related to other facts we know?' And then finally, 'How are these facts applied in a new context.'[145] Throughout the lesson, with repetition, and skillful facilitation by the teacher, students will be able to make these intellectual moves.

The cognitive demand on the students should increase as the lesson progresses. These demand increases are planned and designed to match students' increasing familiarity with the content. If a teacher begins the lesson by asking students the same questions they have planned to ask in the latter portion of the class, then most students will not be ready to respond.

The intentional incremental increase in intellectual demand helps a teacher determine why a particular student may be unable to perform at a higher level during the lesson. Is it because their background knowledge is insufficient? Is it because they do not understand the foundational information? Is it because they need more examples in order to make the cognitive leap? By gradually increasing the level of cognitive engagement, a teacher can more accurately diagnose issues as well as give better instructive and constructive feedback. In other words, by controlling variables the teacher is able to better understand the formative data.

In declarative lessons students do not practice tasks during the lesson that they will be asked to complete independently.[146] At the beginning of the lesson it would be very easy for the teacher to describe the decalarative information

---

144 Willingham, Daniel T. (2002) 'Ask the Cognitive Scientist: Inflexible Knowledge: The first step to expertise', *American Federation of Teachers*. Available at: https://www.aft.org/periodical/american-educator/winter-2002/ask-cognitive-scientist-inflexible-knowledge.

145 Some educators may describe the above as increasing rigor. After reading never ending blog debates about the definition of rigor, I try my darndest not to use that word. Feel free to use it if you like, but I am sticking with 'intellectually demanding.'

146 This in contrast to procedural lessons where the independent practice looks exactly like models which look exactly like the guided practice.

embedded in the learning objective and have the students parrot the it over and over and over again until they have rote learned it. For example, if the lesson objective is to list three causes of the Civil War, have the students repeat these until they are able to recite this information. The problem with that method, of course, is that the students have not learned anything – they will not ultimately understand the main causes of the Civil War.

The teacher should have asked many questions during the lesson that touch on, approximate, probe, and prepare students for completing independent practice, but, the teacher should not ask the specific questions that will be a part of independent practice. Guided practice leads students to be able to successfully complete independent practice. The implication is that there is a clear learning objective and corresponding independent practice.[147] In the sample lesson presented later in this chapter the independent practice is:

> Students will explain why third party presidential candidates appear and why they have not been successful.

During the key ideas and expert thinking (modeling) components of the lesson, checking for understanding questions are qualitatively different from the questions that will be asked during guided practice (see the lesson later in this chapter). The questions early in the lesson are fact based, they are literal: What is a third party candidate? When do third party candidates emerge? Why don't third party candidates win? etc. During declarative lessons, the teacher exerts maximum control by first engaging students at the most literal level before moving on to more esoteric questions.

Once the teacher has ensured that students know the basic facts, it is time to guide the students through tasks that will require them to engage with the subject in a different manner. Cognitive engagement with the concepts increases and deepens throughout the lesson. The teacher will increase student engagement to a more cognitively sophisticated level by asking students to use the literal information to make inferences. For example: a third party candidate may be very popular in certain parts of the country but not in others. Why might that be true?

At this point in the lesson the design task for the teacher is to ask questions and select other tasks that necessitate students to incorporate the initial

---

147 See chapter 3.

fact-based information and use it to make inferences, compare, analyze, etc. This may look very much like a discussion.[148] It may look like one of a variety of activities.

In guided practice the teacher's role changes from instructor to facilitator and coach. The role of the facilitator and coach is to:

1. Prompt and direct students in a manner that will engage them in activities that will foster deeper meaning.
2. Provide constructive and instructive feedback during those activities.
3. Determine if students are ready to be released to independent practice using formative data collected during the activities.
4. Or, if a teacher determines the class is not ready for the next cognitive leap, application, or evaluation, the independent practice can easily be modified to ensure success at a less sophisticated level.

DESIGNING GUIDED PRACTICE

Remember – Understand – Apply

A gradual release in declarative lessons is accomplished by increasing the level of cognitive engagement for the students throughout the lesson. Earlier in the lesson students are asked to remember answers to literal questions about new concepts. Guided practice is the time in the lesson when students begin to use that literal information to make inferences.

There is nothing more fun than designing and facilitating guided practice for declarative lessons. It is the part of the lesson where the teacher's creativity can shine. The only limitations to what can be done during guided practice are the teacher's imagination and time.[149]

---

148 I have observed many teachers who are skilled in leading classroom discussions. However, students can share opinions and debate without approaching the learning objective if the teacher does not guide their answers by demanding they include prior content. The critical formative data you are collecting is knowledge of prior content and basic facts continue to be the focus of the lesson. It is easy to get off track.

149 Remember, you only have about 10-20 minutes of guided practice depending on the age of your students.

The teacher should ask herself:

- After I have presented key ideas and expert thinking, what will the students know?
- What will the students be asked to do in independent practice?
- What is the gap?
- What structured activities can I facilitate that will help students fill that gap?[150]

The good news is that the only limits to what structured activities you choose are your imagination and the time available.[151] The bad news is that sometimes having so much freedom can be overwhelming and paralyzing for the teacher and confusing for the students.

Every teacher needs a list of four or five solid guided practice structured activities that can be used with any content. Four or five structured activities are plenty to incrementally fill gaps and provide enough variety to keep students interested.[152] Having a limited number of structured activities allows students to learn the necessary routines attached to each activity. Like all other classroom procedures repetition and structure will save time.

EXAMPLE OF GUIDED PRACTICE IN A DECLARATIVE LESSON

Phew! That sounds like a lot of gobbledygook. A specific example should help to clarify. Below is a lesson about third party presidential candidates. Because there is so much flexibility in what can be done during guided practice, alternative activities will be listed.

---

150 If you have some type of PLC structure in your school these questions will look familiar.

151 'Activity' is another of those words educators argue about. What is an 'activity'? 'Stuff you do to help kids learn.' What is a 'structured activity'? 'An activity in which the structure stays the same, but the content changes', e.g. comparing and contrasting documents.

152 Some sophisticated concepts may take more time for students to grasp. In these cases both the independent practice and guided practice should look very similar.

Preview

Does anyone remember when the president was not a Democrat or Republican? Who can name the last president who was not a member of one of the major political parties?

Learning objective

Students will explain why third party presidential candidates appear and why they have not been successful.[153]

Review

Here is a list of issues. With your partner, identify which issue(s) is/are usually associated with Republicans, and which issues are associated with Democrats?

- Eliminate the Death Penalty.
- Eliminate Abortion.
- Voting Integrity.

Key ideas

1. Third parties are formed around a particular issue, platform, or personality that is not part of the ideology of either of the major parties.
2. A third party candidate has never been elected to the presidency of the United States, but some minor candidates have been from third parties.
3. A strong third party candidate for president may garner enough votes to affect the outcome of a national election.
4. Policies advocated by third parties may become popular enough to be absorbed into the platform of a major party.

First Level of Cognitive Engagement: Remember (Literal recall of key ideas)

Checking for understanding questions:

---

153 There are a variety of ways students could explain. You get to decide. An essay could work, as could digital slides with an oral presentation, or just an oral presentation, bullet points, a concept map, etc. The only requirements are: (1) The students provide a 'grade-level' explanation, (2) the students already have the skills to produce the essay, slides, presentation, etc.

- *What is a third party candidate?*
- *Why do we have third party candidates?*
- *What are some third party issues?*
- *When do we have third party candidates?*

Commentary: All the checking for understanding questions come directly from the key ideas. The questions are low level recall questions.

Explain expert thinking
Use concept map: Cause – Effect

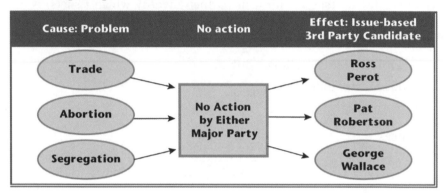

Language frame:

Because of the lack of legislative action on (topic) a third party candidate (name) emerged.

Causes/social/economic issues that cause third party candidates.

Effects on issues for major parties.

Checking for understanding questions:

What is a third party candidate?

When do third party candidates emerge?

What are some historical third party candidate issues?

Next Level of Cognitive Engagement: Understand (make inferences)

What has the impact of third party candidates on the issues been?

How could a losing third party candidate impact the outcome of an election?

Commentary: The last two questions 'raise the stakes' for students. Describing the impacts is more cognitively engaging than the first three questions.[154] But, students will not be able to answer the last two questions if they are not able to answer the more basic questions. The demand for cognitive engagement is gradually increasing.

Guided practice

With a partner use the following websites to answer the questions below.

Video Clip: 'The History of Third Party Candidates in Presidential Elections' (https://www.c-span.org/classroom/document/?16933).

Article: 'Here's How Third-Party Candidates Have Changed Elections' (https://www.history.com/news/third-party-candidates-election-influence-facts).

There is a tremendous disparity in wealth distribution in the US. Do you think that could give rise to a third party? If a third party emerges, will that draw votes away from Democrats or Republicans?

Many Americans have lost jobs due to factories moving overseas. Do you think that could give rise to a third party? If a third party emerges, will that draw votes away from Democrats or Republicans?

The US has been fighting wars for many years. Do you think that could give rise to a third party? If a third party emerges, will that draw votes away from Democrats or Republicans?

Commentary: Again, the tasks raise the 'cognitive stakes' for the students, demanding that they analyze and evaluate. The students must utilize the facts and concepts from the review through expert thinking components of the lesson to do the assigned tasks in the guided practice.

---

154 Teachers should be prepared to 'raise the stakes' but without feeling pressured that students are able to answer the next level questions. Remain focused on the learning objective and independent practice. There is always tomorrow.

Alternative guided practice #1

With a partner: each partner reads one of two articles and notes important information. Then the partners compare notes and list similarities and differences in the articles.

Alternative Guided Practice #2

Students watch a short video about a third party candidate. Students are divided into two groups. One group represents Democrats and the group represents Republicans. Students in each group respond to the third party candidate in the video from their party's perspective.

Additional possible guided practice activities

Have students read from the text with questions to guide them.

Read primary source documents identifying third party issues.

Do an 'Iron Chef' using a variety of possible sources.[155]

Compare and contrast primary documents.

Compare and contrast primary and secondary source documents.

Watch a video about a third party candidate – identify third party issues.

Lead a discussion about third party issues.

Create ads for third party candidates.

Create attack ads against third party candidates.

Teachers' creativity can shine in creating activities, but too much creativity can be distracting (see extraneous cognitive load, chapter 3). Have four or five 'go to moves' that the students are familiar with. You don't want to be teaching a new activity or app every time you have new content. Tick tock, tick tock.

Closure

What was the learning objective?

What is a third party candidate?

---

155 For 'Iron Chef', see Hebern, M. & Corippo, J. (2018) *Eduprotocol: Field guide book 1.* San Diego, CA, Dave Burgess.

When do third party candidates emerge?

What are third party candidate issues?

What have the impacts of third party candidates on these issues been?

What have the impacts of third party candidates on elections been?

Commentary: closure includes questions from the learning objective, key ideas, and expert thinking. The questions cover remembering and understanding. These questions represent the content that the teacher deemed the 'gap' from the facts presented in key ideas to application in independent practice.

Next Level of Cognitive Engagement: Apply

Independent Practice
Analyze an article about a third party candidate. Include in your analysis the social and economic issues that gave rise to the candidate and how their candidacy might impact each of the two major parties.

DESIGN TIPS

Tip #1. Prepare inferential, higher order, questions before the lesson

All students are able to move from *remembering* literal information to *understanding*, making inferences, to *applying* concepts if they are guided by the right questions. It is relatively easy to think of literal questions 'on the fly'. What is a third party candidate? Why do third party candidates emerge? etc. It is much more difficult to come up with questions that will spur higher order thinking.

Prepare lots of questions that are inferential. How many do you need? A lot. We never know which question will help a student make that cognitive leap. Have more than you think you will need.

Tip #2. Think of gaps

What does a student know at this point in the lesson? What does he need to know by the end of the lesson? Will the task that I have planned bridge that gap? What questions will help guide their thinking?

Tip #3. Know the end game

All lessons should lead to something. They are a part of a unit, or they are a prerequisite lesson, or it is simply a concept that takes more than one day to understand. Some concepts may take some students a little longer to fully grasp. *Relax.* You can hit it again tomorrow.

DELIVERY TIPS

Tip #1. Continue to reinforce the concept

It is every teacher's dream that students are engaged with academic content. However, don't be fooled by engagement. Depending on the topic, it is very likely that students will be excited, maybe even emotional about a lesson. While it may be exciting for teachers to observe students being so involved in class discussions, it is important that the teacher continue to bring students back to the learning objective at hand.

For example, in the third party candidate lesson above. What if a third party candidate emerged on a platform of stopping all immigration. It is easy to imagine the class being derailed by a lively discussion about immigration (instead of how a third party candidate emerged because of the immigration issue).

How would the teacher continue to reinforce the concept? Be sure to ask questions and make comments that reflect the key ideas. Is there a geographic component to the support for the candidate? From which party would the candidate be likely to take votes? etc. These types of questions allow for the discussion of issues while managing to stay focussed on the learning objective.[156]

---

156 I observed a 1st grade teacher who had decided to use a song to reinforce a concept her kids had learned. In addition to singing, students moved around in a circle in time to the music. The students were walking and singing and were fully engaged in the joy of the music. The teacher stopped the music, got the students' attention, and said, 'I am glad you are having fun, but remember why we are singing this song. Listen to the words. Pay attention to the words.' She started the music again. The students continued to enjoy singing and moving to the music, but they were refocused on the words that reinforced the learning objective.

Tip #2: Enough is enough

When students are really engaged during guided practice it is tempting to just allow them to continue. Remember, guided practice has two goals: (1) for students to practice and engage with the content and (2) for the teacher to gather formative data.

If students are engaged during guided practice – and if you have followed the advice in Tip #1 – then they will continue to be engaged when directed to the independent practice task. If the lesson has been properly designed then the independent practice will be the logical next step to channel their excitement and engagement. They should be ready to roll.

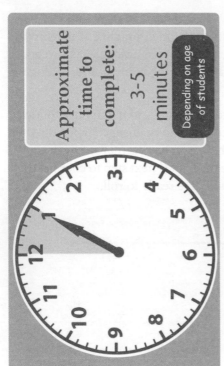

Approximate
time to
complete:
3-5
minutes

Depending on age
of students

COMPONENT CONNECTIONS

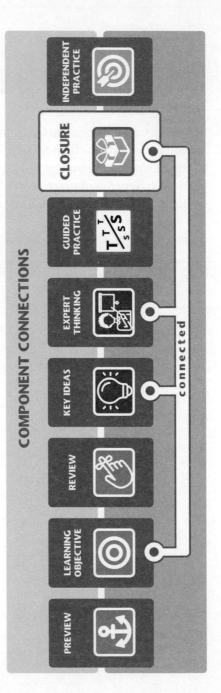

PREVIEW

LEARNING
OBJECTIVE

REVIEW

KEY IDEAS

EXPERT
THINKING

GUIDED
PRACTICE

CLOSURE

INDEPENDENT
PRACTICE

connected

CHAPTER 8
CLOSURE

Big ideas in closure:

- Closure is the final check for understanding before independent practice.
- It reconnects the learning objective, key ideas, and expert thinking.
- Like the review, the teacher asks or prompts, but the students do the work.
- Recall to relearn, i.e. retrieval practice.

OVERVIEW

When teachers are asked to self-report which lesson component is most frequently omitted from a lesson, far and away the most frequent answer is closure.[157] The most frequently reported reasons given by teachers as to why closure is omitted are:

---

157 This reporting is elicited before our training program has shared any understanding of what an effective closure would be, or made any argument made for including it. Whatever teachers think closure is, or whether or not they know why it is important, many are willing to admit without embarrassment to not including it in lessons.

- The time gets away from me.
- Something always seems to come up.
- I simply forget.

These reasons are all just variations on the theme of, 'I say it is important, but I don't really believe it is important.'

Why is closure important? If students are not asked to recall and apply information during closure, they are being robbed of opportunities to learn and master content. An effective closure takes place during the second high retention time (OWL 2). This means that retrieval of information by students, combined with clarifying feedback by the teacher, interact to improve both understanding and retention of lesson content.

Is closure important? Only if you want the students to learn and remember the concepts and skills in your lesson! Closure is the final check for understanding, the last bit of formative data before students are released to independent practice. It will allow the teacher to ensure that students have the proper contextual understanding of concepts and skills in the lesson. Teachers frequently discover that the students' understanding of the lesson is off by 'just a click.' By providing instructive and constructive feedback to students during closure the teacher can be confident the students are ready to benefit from independent practice.

When the relationships of all the lesson components are understood, design and delivery of closure is both efficient and effective. An effective closure is closely tied to other components to provide coherent and cohesive instruction. A properly designed and executed closure will demand that students recall the learning objective, the key ideas (concepts), and the expert thinking (skills). When closure is viewed as a critical part of a well-designed and delivered lesson, teachers will find the time for closure.

As stated previously, students must be actively engaged and prompted to 'perform' in order to learn. Performing, in its most simple terms, means to actually do something. Performance tasks in closure can be answering questions, solving problems, explaining procedures, etc. Everything that teachers have learned about effective checking for understanding needs to be implemented during closure. As a reminder, effective checking for understanding includes:

◻ Adequate wait time.

◻ Checking all students.

◻ Constructive and instructive feedback.

◻ Determine *which* students *do not* know the information.

◻ Determine 'what' information the students *do not know.*

As in the review component of the lesson, it is the students who are doing the work by responding to questions and prompts. Closure is never the teacher saying, 'Students, let me tell you what we learned today.' This point cannot be emphasized too much or too often.

Every time students must apply new concepts and skills they create or enhance learning and memory pathways. Every time students must recall and use information from long-term memory, they are closer to the fluency and mastery that contribute to easy retrieval from long-term memory.

Important! Closure occurs *before* independent practice. Closure is sandwiched in between guided practice and independent practice. Any misconceptions regarding content in the lesson can be cleared up before students practice independently. Because closure occurs after guided practice and before independent practice, performance with feedback reinforces the concepts and skills in the lesson.[158]

Before students are released to independent practice, teachers must ensure that they are able to perform effectively. Closure is the final opportunity for the teacher to decide which students are ready to benefit from independent practice and which students need immediate classroom intervention.

After guided practice has been completed, the teacher should ask, 'Does anyone have any questions?' If the answer is yes, the teacher answers the students' questions. If the answer is no, then say, 'Well I have some questions for you. And, don't forget to use your language frames when you answer.'

DESIGN TIPS

Tip #1. Keep it consistent

Teaching is difficult enough. Don't make it more difficult than it needs to

---

158 Closure occurs during OWL 2 (Optimal Window for Learning 2), a high retention time (see chapter 3).

be by trying to reinvent the wheel for each lesson. An effective closure will contain at least one question from the following three lesson components:

- Learning objective.
- Key ideas.
- Expert thinking.

There should be one or more questions from each of these lesson components in turn. The two major considerations during closure are time and the ages of the students. Closure should not take more than 5-6 minutes and in many cases about half that amount of time.

The younger the students, the less complex the questions need to be. For example, instead of asking 'What was our learning objective today?' If the learning objective was to identify alliteration in a poem, the closure questions for the learning objective might be, 'What did we learn to identify today?' and 'What type of writing did we use to find alliteration?'

Use these three questions as language frames and as a starting point for designing an effective closure for all your lessons.

- Learning objective: 'What was our learning objective?'
- Key idea: 'What is a _____?'
- Expert thinking: 'How do you _____?'

In most cases, teachers can use the same checking for understanding questions they used during the lesson while initially teaching those components. Answers to checking for understanding questions earlier in the lesson are usually lower-level questions that only require recitation of information. For example, at the beginning of the lesson when the teacher asks students, 'What is our learning objective?' Students are able to answer because the learning objective is written on the board and is visible to the class. Students are able to read and answer the teacher's question, but they really have no understanding of what the learning objective means. During closure, the questions may be the same, but the students' answers will be more insightful.

Students answering the same questions during closure have had the benefit of interacting with the content and practicing skills in various contexts during the lesson. Students will not only be able to read what the learning objective is, they will also be able to discuss and explain it in depth when prompted by the teacher.

Tip #2. Write your questions when you plan the lesson

In addition to questions that may have been previously asked during the lesson, you can develop additional and different questions that may be used specifically during closure. Even if these questions are different those used earlier in the class, they should test the same information. For example:

- Learning objective: 'If your parents ask you what you learned in math today, what will you tell them?'
- Learning objective (early grades): 'We just learned a new way to add. What is the name of that new way?'
- Key ideas: 'How is _____different from _____?'
- Key ideas: 'How do you identify a _____?'
- Key ideas: 'I used to think _____. Now I think _____.'
- Expert thinking: 'Pretend your partner was not here for this lesson. Teach her how to answer the following question.'
- Expert thinking: 'Here is a completed example. Identify the mistake if there is one.'

Although these questions do not seem sophisticated, it can be difficult to create new questions on the fly.

DELIVERY TIPS

Tip #1. Closure is for all students

Teachers do not do the closure. Teachers do not tell. Teachers ask questions. Teachers direct students to perform tasks. Teachers facilitate closure, students do the work.

Ask yourself, 'Which students need to know this material?' The answer, of course, is all of them! With that in mind, be sure to use all the rules for checking for understanding to promote equitable opportunities for all students to respond to prompts and questions.[159]

Tip #2. Closure is active for students

Closure is not the teacher recapping the lesson for the class. As stated earlier in this chapter, one of the central purposes of closure is to provide

---

159 See appendix III.

retrieval practice for students. Closure and review work in a very similar way. Teachers create demands through questions to support and reinforce proper encoding of information into long-term memory by practicing recall.

If the teacher simply tells the class the important details of the lesson, she robs the students of another opportunity to 'recall and learn' through the act of retrieval.

Tip #3. Be efficient, be quick

When designed properly, using questions that are phrased in the manner described in this chapter, closure should take no longer than five minutes. In most instances, less than five minutes.

If your data tells you to pull an intervention group, be sure to re-teach and practice only the necessary discrete areas. Do not reteach the entire lesson. All of us, but especially struggling students, like to perform tasks they already know how to perform. Focus on the discrete new content in the lesson that students need to practice.

NOTES FRO/M THE FIELD

A district instructional coach reported that she had planned and taught a lesson for a 4th grade class. Prior to this lesson, the coach's teaching experience had been limited to secondary students. Because the coach was not familiar with the grade-level or this particular class, the most difficult part of designing the lesson was selecting appropriate content for the students.

The coach chose to teach a lesson on the California State Constitution. As soon as she began to teach the lesson, the coach realized that the students did not have the background knowledge that the regular classroom teacher had claimed they had.

The coach taught the lesson. The students were excited, student participation was good, and many students were able to answer questions during the lesson. The coach thought she had weathered the storm regarding lack of content knowledge.

When the coach asked the closure questions, it was clear the objectives from the lesson had not been met. She was disappointed that the students were not able to get more from this lesson. She was happy she had included closure and determined that students would be unable to complete the planned independent practice.

Having clear objectives and targets allows student data to be analyzed in the proper context. To paraphrase, and rephrase, the often-misquoted Lewis Carroll, 'If you don't know where you are going then you can easily be fooled into thinking you got somewhere.'[160]

FREQUENTLY ASKED QUESTIONS

Q: Can I use an exit ticket as closure?

A: Closure is a check for understanding that provides (1) the teacher with data, (2) an opportunity to give immediate feedback to students. An exit ticket provides the teacher with data, but gives no opportunity to provide feedback. By definition, an exit ticket means the students have exited. The exit ticket falls short as closure.

Q: We are an AVID school. Can I use the AVID summary as closure?

A: Absolutely! Prior to having students write their summaries ask them the closure questions so you can give feedback. Tell them a good summary of the lesson should include the learning objective, key ideas, and expert thinking. The inclusion of that information will provide the students with a nice template for their summaries.

Q: When I tell students to teach each other I often hear students using the exact words I used during the lesson. Should I have them paraphrase?

A: No. Feel honored that your students paid such close attention. Good job! Having students paraphrase too early in the learning process is a mistake.

---

160 "'Cheshire Puss ... would you tell me, please, which way I ought to go from here?'" "That depends a good deal on where you want to get to", said the Cat. "I don't much care where...", said Alice. "Then it doesn't matter which way you go", said the Cat. "...so long as I get SOMEWHERE", Alice added as an explanation. "Oh, you're sure to do that", said the Cat, "if you only walk long enough.'"

Approximate
time to
complete:
5-20
minutes

Depending on age
of students

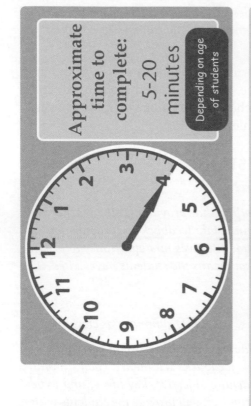

COMPONENT CONNECTIONS

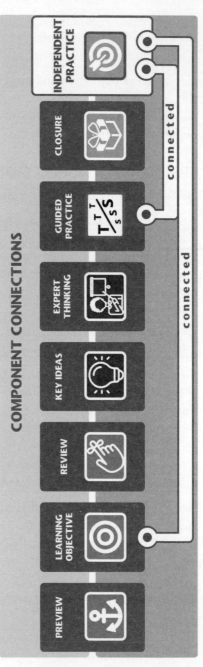

PREVIEW

LEARNING
OBJECTIVE

REVIEW

KEY IDEAS

EXPERT
THINKING

GUIDED
PRACTICE

CLOSURE

INDEPENDENT
PRACTICE

connected

connected

CHAPTER 9
INDEPENDENT PRACTICE

Big ideas in independent practice:

- Independent practice matches the learning objective exactly.
- In procedural lessons it matches the expert thinking and guided practice.
- In declarative lessons expert thinking and guided practice lead to a more cognitively engaging task.

OVERVIEW

There are two parts to learning. The first part is the instruction provided by the teacher. The second is adequate practice by the student. Independent practice is exactly what it says: an opportunity for students to independently apply the concepts and skills that were taught in the lesson.

Effective lessons have just the right amount of new content. Effective lessons include adequate amounts of practice during a high retention time (i.e. OWL 2). This helps to accelerate the process of moving new learning from working memory into long-term memory. Content metaphorically migrates to long-term memory with the help of effective practice and sufficient repetitions to attain proficiency and automaticity.

It is not unusual for students to be assigned more independent practice than is necessary. The number of independent repetitions that are necessary on the first day of instruction is about eight. Over time, students need many more repetitions. The number of successful repetitions students need over time may be as many as 40. These repetitions can be in various forms and contexts. But, on the first day, following initial instruction, eight repetitions are sufficient.

Getting additional repetitions is relatively easy because of the recursive and linear nature of most curricula. In most cases additional repetitions are either embedded in new content or become constituent skills in new content.

As with guided practice, the design and delivery of independent practice will vary based on whether the lesson is procedural (something to do), or declarative (something to know). Below is a discussion on how to align independent practice, exactly, in both types of lessons.

PROCEDURAL LESSONS

Everything matches exactly

Expert thinking matches guided practice. The context of the review matches exactly to how skills are used. Guided practice matches independent practice. By making sure there is an exact match throughout the lesson, teachers can be assured that students will be able complete independent practice.

There is one caveat, or clarification. Practice problems should match the guided practice exactly, but this does not preclude the inclusion of problems that have previously learned concepts embedded in them. It is fine, even good, to include such problems. Indeed this is one way that teachers can distribute the practice of skills and concepts across lessons to get the necessary additional repetitions to reach automaticity. Providing such distributed practice helps provide reinforcement of prior learned skills as well as forcing students to slow down and concentrate on conditional knowledge.[161]

Do not trust the textbook

Publishers are infamous for including problems in the problem sets that do not match the learning objective. The argument for including problems that do not match is to 'provide a challenge' to students. Students *do* need to be challenged, but not as they are learning a new skill. Check the problem set to be sure all problems assigned match the learning objective.

Do not assign independent practice too soon

After closure, students who have demonstrated during the lesson that they are ready for independent practice should begin at once.[162] Students who have not demonstrated they are ready should receive immediate intervention.[163]

Do not overdo

Eight repetitions is enough on the first day of learning a new skill.

DECLARATIVE LESSONS

Practice approximately matches

The expert thinking approximates what will be done during guided practice but it does not match exactly. Guided practice approximates independent practice, but it does not match exactly. Because these questions and checks for understanding approximate tasks at the next stage of the lesson, teachers must make a judgement as to whether or not students are able to move to the independent practice.

---

161 If students are assigned problems from previous lessons then how to recognize when to use a particular procedure (i.e. conditional knowledge) must be emphasized.

162 If students are not able to perform the entire procedure you may want to assign the parts of it that students are able to perform. Many times when students are learning new skills they are able to perform all the steps except one. In that case have students independently practice multiple problems up to that particular step.

163 Elementary teachers are experts at 'pulling a group.' High school teachers are generally less apt to pull a group for immediate intervention for a couple of reasons. First, managing groups is not a skill that is emphasized during pre-service training for secondary teachers. Second, most secondary teachers teach to the bell and don't allow time for intervention.

No new skills

The focus of declarative lessons is the learning of new conceptual and/or conditional knowledge. During a declarative lesson teachers do not model how to perform the independent practice, but rather how they think about the content. Students should already possess any skills necessary to perform the independent practice. For example, if the independent practice is to write an essay comparing and contrasting the two political parties, students should already possess the skill of writing a compare and contrast essay. If the independent practice is to compare and contrast the two political parties using a double-bubble concept map, then students should already know how to use a double-bubble map etc.

DESIGN TIPS FOR INDEPENDENT PRACTICE

Tip #1. Independent practice is either the first or second planning decision

The purpose of this component is to practice concepts and skills taught in the lesson. Remember the planning order? First, the learning objective then independent practice.[164] Make sure the independent practice matches the learning objective exactly. Otherwise you may have taught the greatest lesson, with students cognitively engaged and exceptional checking for understanding, but the students might still not able to successfully complete the independent practice.

Tip #2. Do not trust the textbook

Test the independent practice problem set provided in the text. Like the guided practice, you must make sure you select problems that can be solved using the processes taught. You are still the boss of the book!

DELIVERY TIPS FOR INDEPENDENT PRACTICE

Tip #1. Do not assign independent practice if students are not ready

If the formative assessment data during guided practice and closure tells you that the majority of the students will not be successful doing the

---

164 See chapter 3. Technically, you could choose the independent practice first and then infer the learning objective.

independent practice then do not assign it. Reflect, regroup, and reteach. You can always have students practice something they already know. This is far preferable to having them practice incorrectly.

Tip #2. Pull a group for immediate intervention

If a large majority of the class is ready for independent practice then assign it to those students. The remainder of the class needs immediate intervention to remediate whatever part of the lesson is unclear. It has been my experience that if the lesson has been designed and delivered properly this group of students will be relatively small. Usually the number of students to be remediated varies from 2-6 students.[165]

The immediate intervention is usually brief because the teacher knows exactly what the students do not know, or cannot do. The entire lesson is not retaught: only those parts in which the students struggled. Because the group is small the teacher is able to provide more personalized attention and feedback.

When students are being remediated after a lesson, then appropriate scaffolds will be used. Let's assume the learning objective in the lesson was to compute percentages. One of the steps in the procedure will be to multiply. If students do not know their math facts, the teacher would provide scaffolding by performing those calculations. The teacher already knows the students do not know their math facts. Performing the calculations in this instance will allow students to focus on the new concept or skill. At some time later during the school day the teacher must then facilitate effective practice for those students until they learn their math facts. When you have pulled a group of students for remediation in calculating percentages, that is not the time to practice math facts.

NOTES FROM THE FIELD

After closure a high school language arts teacher did a check-in with students asking them to self-report their confidence in their ability to complete the assigned independent practice. The students were asked to

---

165 One teacher coined the phrase, 'I am going to "kidney" the students who don't get it.' This meant the students were called to the back of the room to sit at the teacher's kidney shaped table for immediate intervention.

judge their level of comfort as: (1) really got it, (2) do not have a clue, or (3) somewhere in between.

Students who answered '1' moved to the back of the room and began their independent practice assignment. Students who self-reported '2' or '3' were directed to move to a row of desks adjacent to the whiteboard.

After the students had relocated to the appropriate desks, the teacher re-taught only those parts of the lesson that she knew were problematic. The teacher knew which parts of the lesson needed to be re-taught based on the student data generated during the lesson. The teacher did not reteach the entire lesson.

While debriefing with the teacher subsequent to the lesson, I complimented her on pulling a group to immediately provide intervention. I told her I had seen hundreds of high school lessons and she was the first high school teacher I had ever seen that pulled a group – although we always recommend doing so during our initial training.[166]

The teacher was surprised that I had never seen a high school teacher pull a group. She said, 'Every conference I have ever attended recommends that the teacher provide intervention immediately to those students who need it.'

FREQUENTLY ASKED QUESTIONS

Q: What do I do with students who finish their independent practice while I am still working with a small group of students?

A: What are your current procedures for students who finish work? Do they read? Do other homework? If you do not have a procedure that informs students what to do when they complete their work, it is not too soon to develop one.

Q: Is it okay to assign students 'challenge problems'?

A: It depends. Are the problems challenging because the content has not been taught? If that is the case, then hold off. Are the problems challenging because they involve larger numbers or constituent skills that all the students have not yet mastered? Then allow students to try them, but do not require them.

---

166 Pulling intervention groups is very common in elementary.

CHAPTER 10
WRAP UP

I remember a phone conversation that I had with a colleague when we were first grappling with the FAST Framework. My colleague asked, 'If a teacher could only use one component of the FAST Framework during a lesson, which do you think would be the most important?' Off the top of my head my response was, 'Expert thinking. If a teacher models effectively then students would at least have a fighting chance to complete the independent practice.' Nearly as quickly as I had responded I then added, 'But without having a clear learning objective, the teacher would not have selected the appropriate independent practice, which in turn would have dictated the proper guided practice, which then would have led the teacher to decide on the best content to model.'

Now, nearly two decades later, which do I believe is the most important component of FAST Framework? There is no single 'most important' component. The power of the FAST Framework is that its components are cohesive, coherent, and interrelated. As much as I hate clichés and buzzwords, the proper word to use here is 'synergy': 'the whole is greater than the sum of its parts'.[167] That is what makes the lessons clear and accessible to students. The preview helps the students connect the new lesson to prior knowledge, which makes the learning objective understandable, which leads to the review, etc.

FINAL REVIEW
This is a final review of each component and of how they relate to each other. It is also a final review of the most important tactical objectives and

---

167 Yes, I know, another cliché.

key considerations in both the design and delivery of each component. This review will be done in the order that most lessons are taught; the order the FAST Framework is presented in the planning document (see chapter 1).

Preview

The preview is related to the key ideas and closure. It connects the students' prior knowledge to the key ideas and concepts of the lesson. The questions that the teacher asks to prompt students during the preview may also be asked again during closure to anchor concepts.

Important things to keep in mind when designing the preview:

- It must connect to prior knowledge for all students.
- This prior knowledge is not necessarily derived from the classroom.
- The context of the prior knowledge must match the context of the lesson.

Important things to keep in mind when delivering the preview:

- Keep the preview short. Most preview connections can be made within 1-3 minutes.
- All students should connect past experiences mentally, but they all do not need to share these with the entire class.
- Questions regarding the students' connections to the key ideas in the lesson should be focused on the relationship between prior knowledge and the new key ideas.

Learning objective

The learning objective is directly related to the independent practice. It is also related to the guided practice, and will be part of the closure.

The learning objective provides focus for the lesson and drives the content and all subsequent components to the independent practice. Embedded in a learning objective will always be a concept and a skill that students will use to demonstrate their understanding of the key idea(s).

The learning objective should be clearly stated by the teacher and students. It should be written and remain visible during the lesson.

Important considerations when designing the learning objective:

- Teach only one objective at a time.[168]
- The learning objective must match independent practice exactly.
- It should be simply written.

Important considerations when delivering the learning objective:

- The learning objective should be visible throughout the lesson.
- Students should acknowledge and read the learning objective. This should be kept brief as students will not yet understand what the objective means.
- Return to the objective throughout the lesson.

Review

The review is related to expert thinking and the necessary constituent skills needed to perform the new skill in the lesson. The review provides recall practice for the necessary constituent skills and knowledge.

Important things to keep in mind when designing the review:

- It connects prior learned academic knowledge to the new lesson.
- It connects prior skills to the new skills in the lesson.
- Students perform the review by answering teacher queries.
- The content and context of the review is determined by what skills students will need to be successful in the lesson.

Important considerations when delivering the review:

- Time is limited to 3-4 minutes.
- Students respond to questions and/or problems posed by the teacher.
- The teacher asks. The teacher does not tell.
- Questions must engage all students.

---

168 Remember! The most frequently observed reason for students not performing well during lessons is the teacher attempting to teach too much. A learning objective that has a single focus will help solve that problem.

Key ideas

The key ideas component is related to preview and closure. It is the conceptual part of the lesson.

Important considerations when designing the key ideas component of the lesson:

- There is always conceptual knowledge in a lesson.
- The amount of content should be limited.
- Concepts include both declarative and conditional knowledge.
- This is when concept maps and language frames are introduced.
- 'What' precedes 'how' in the learning sequence.
- Include definitions, examples, and non-examples. Non-examples may not be appropriate with very young students.

Important considerations when delivering the key ideas component of the lesson:

- Time limited by OWL 1.
- Students use and practice language frames.
- Tie key ideas to preview.

Expert thinking

Expert thinking is related to review and closure. It is the modeling portion of the lesson. During a lesson that focuses on a procedure, the teacher explains her thinking on how to perform that procedure. During declarative lessons, the teacher explains how she thinks about a concept.

Important considerations when designing the expert thinking component of the lesson:

- Expert thinking is modeling.
- Expert thinking about a skill is how to solve a problem.
- Expert thinking about a concept is how to organize information.
- Not all modeling is created equal.

Important considerations when delivering expert thinking:

- Limit examples to two (Whole – Part – Whole).

- No questions to, or from students.
- Leave at least one example visible to students throughout the lesson.

Guided practice/gradual release

Guided practice is directly related to independent practice, which is related to the learning objective, which is related to the key ideas … which is related to expert thinking.

Guided practice is the first time students have an opportunity to practice the new content.

Important considerations when designing the guided practice:

- Develop a step-by-step procedure for procedural lessons.
- Concepts should be embedded in procedures.
- Develop a concept map and language frame for declarative lessons.
- Plan for the gradual release to occur over three repetitions.

Important considerations when delivering guided practice:

- Students are immediately doing 100% of the work.
- It provides formative data to guide remainder of lesson.
- Instructive and constructive feedback is provided to the whole class.

Closure

Closure is related to the learning objective, key ideas, expert thinking, and guided practice. The teacher asks questions about prior components of the lesson, i.e. it is the final check for understanding.

Important considerations when designing closure:

- It is the final check for understanding before independent practice.
- Ask questions from the learning objective, key ideas, and expert thinking.

Important considerations when delivering closure:

- The teacher asks, the students perform.
- It is retrieval practice for all students.

- Correct any misconceptions at this time.
- At this point determine which students proceed to independent practice and which students will receive immediate in-class intervention.

Independent practice

Independent practice is related to all components. It provides the focus for all other components. Independent practice is when students begin the necessary repetitions needed to make new learning permanent.

Considerations when designing independent practice:

- It matches the learning objective exactly.
- In procedural lessons it matches the expert thinking and guided practice.
- In declarative lessons it incorporates content from the expert thinking and guided practice into a cognitively more engaging task.
- Plan for 8 repetitions.

Considerations when delivering independent practice:

- Do not assign it if the majority of a class are not ready.
- Pull a small group for immediate classroom intervention.

FINAL WORD

The FAST Framework is not 'another tool in your toolbox'. It *is* your toolbox. This framework has been crafted to help design lessons that complement how students learn. It applies to all learning and should be utilized for instructing students in any new content.

This framework is a mind-set. The more frequently it is implemented, the more quickly it becomes a meta-learning tool for students. Some have disparaged the FAST Framework as being so structured that it takes the fun out of learning. Where is the imagination? Where is the fun in lessons that lack the bells and whistles that students love?

The fun of learning is learning. Never forget that!

APPENDIX I
CONCEPT MAPS AND LANGUAGE FRAMES

CONCEPT MAPS

Concept maps are visual representations of the ways that we think about concepts and relate them to each other. The most frequent and common conceptual relationships are:

1. Attributes: identifying, explaining, and/or describing an object or concept based on what it is made up of.
2. Categorizing: how an object or idea is a subset of a larger category.
3. Compare and Contrast: how ideas or objects are similar or different.
4. Sequencing: how ideas relate to other ideas in time.
5. Cause and Effect: given an event, what is a necessary antecedent, and what necessarily follows.
6. Cycles: cycles are a combination of sequencing, as one event follows another, and cause and effect, as each event contains a causal element that necessarily leads to the next.

Notice that there are only six concept maps that you and your students need to learn. In any given week you may encounter a gazillion different concepts maps in your textbooks, but you only need these six. Before using these concept maps to aid in teaching academic content to students, they must be instructed in the use of each of them. The students should practice using each concept map with information that they already know (e.g. What are the attributes of a playground? Compare and contrast hot dogs and hamburgers, etc.). Teaching students how to use the maps using content they already know allows them to focus on learning how the concept maps work. After the students are comfortable with the concept maps themselves, you can begin to use them to teach new academic concepts.

LANGUAGE FRAMES

If concept maps are visual representations of concepts then language frames provide a linguistic structure that puts words to them.

When a writer presents an idea, the structure of their writing is dictated by whether they are discussing attributes, categorizing, comparing and contrasting, sequencing, showing cause and effect, or describing a cycle. The concept maps reflect these text structures; therefore it is easy to create language frames that provide a structure for the articulation of concepts for students.

Imagine constructing a paragraph to describe the information in a concept map that categorizes mathematical operations. The topic sentence describing this concept map might be something like: 'The four mathematical operations are addition, subtraction, multiplication, and division.' Guess what. You just constructed a language frame for categorizing! Each concept map will provide the structure for a similar sentence.

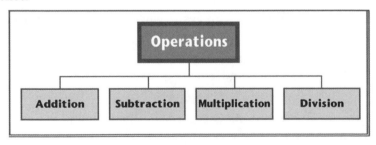

Language frame for categorizing map:

There are _____ types of _____. They are _____ , _____ , _____ , and _____ .

I recommend you have a concept map and language frame wall in your classroom. An example of each map and its corresponding language frame should remain displayed to provide an anchor for students throughout the year.

THE CONCEPT MAPS

The concept maps are representations of how we think, speak, and write. As such they may well resemble other graphic organizers you may have encountered in the past – as you read about each of them you may say to yourself, 'Oh, that is a Frayer!', or, 'That is a thinking map.'

Below are three examples each of our six concept maps and their corresponding language frames. The first example is blank and shows the basic format of each map. The second illustrates non-academic content that might be used to teach the map format itself (e.g. the attributes of a 'playground'). The third uses academic content to demonstrate the map and language frame's classroom application (e.g. the attributes of 'decomposers' from life science).

Attribute concept map

The attribute concept map is used to list multiple characteristics of a concept or entity. The concept or entity being described is placed in the middle circle and the descriptions are placed in each box.

Attribute map (blank):

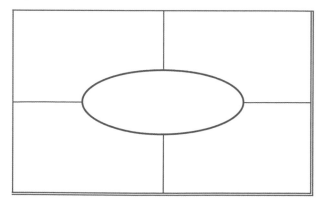

Language frame for attribute map (blank):

I know this is a _____ because it has a _____,
a_____, a _____, and a _____ .

Attribute map for playground (non-academic):

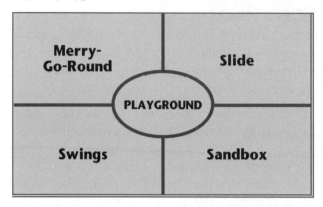

Language frame for playground attribute map (non-academic):

I know that it is a <u>playground</u> because it has a <u>merry-go-round</u>, <u>swings</u>, <u>slide</u>, and a <u>sandbox</u>.

Attribute map for decomposers (academic):

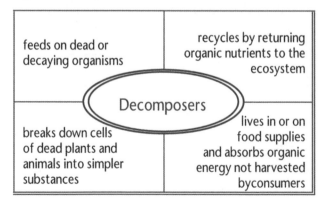

Language frame for decomposers attribute map (academic):

I know that an <u>earthworm</u> is a <u>decomposer</u> because it <u>feeds on dead or decaying organisms</u>, <u>recycles by returning organic nutrients to the</u>

ecosystem, breaks down the cells of dead plants and animals into simpler substances, and lives in or on food supplies and absorbs organic energy not harvested by consumers.

Categorizing concept map

Language frame for categorizing map (blank):

There are _____ types of _____ . They are _____ , _____ , and _____ .

Categorizing map for cars (non- academic):

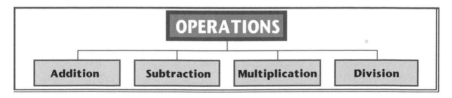

Language frame for categorizing cars map (non-academic):

There are three types of cars. They are gas, electric, and hybrid.

Categorizing map for math operations (academic):

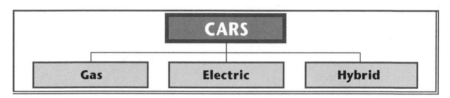

Language frame for categorizing math operations map:

There are four mathematical operations. They are addition, subtraction, multiplication, and division.

Compare and contrast concept map

In this concept map format the two things being compared and contrasted are placed in the circles to the right and left.

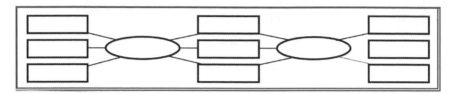

Language frame for compare and contrast map (blank):

_____ are the same as _____ because _____. They are different because _____ and _____ _____.

Compare and contrast map for hot dogs and hamburgers (non-academic):

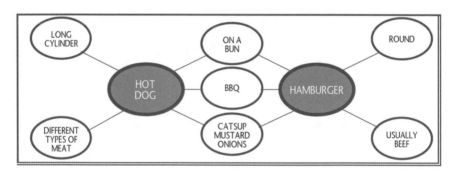

Language frame for compare and contrast hot dogs and hamburgers map (non-academic):

Hot dogs are the same as hamburgers because both are served in a bun, are barbecued, and are served with catsup, mustard, and onions. They are different because hot dogs are a long cylinder shape and have different types of meat and a hamburger is round and is usually beef.

Compare and contrast concept map for fables and folktales (academic):

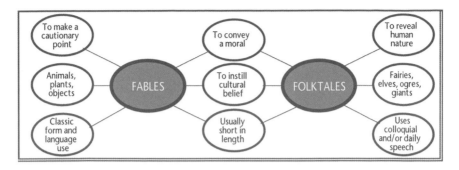

Language frame for compare and contrast fables and folktales map (academic):

Fables are the same as folktales because they are usually short and they convey a moral to instill a cultural belief. They are different because fables feature animals, plants, and other inanimate objects and folktales feature make believe characters and use use colloquial speech.

Sequence concept map

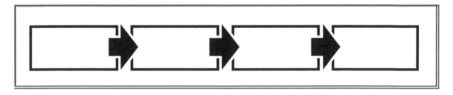

Language frame for sequence map (blank);

The first _____ is _____. Next, _____ .
Then_____. And finally _____ .

Sequence map for daily activities (non-academic):

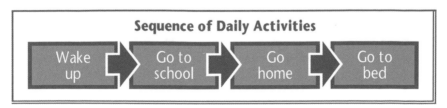

Language frame daily activities (non-academic):

The first thing <u>I do every day</u> is <u>wake up</u>. Next, <u>I go to school</u>. Then <u>I go home</u>. And finally, <u>I go to bed</u>.

Sequence map identifying images as symbols (academic):

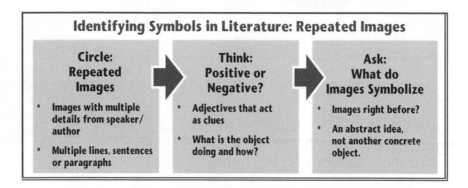

Language frame for indentifying images as symbols map (academic):

When I <u>identify repeated images as symbols</u> the first thing I do is <u>circle the repeated images</u>. Next, <u>I think, are the images positive or negative</u>? And, finally <u>I ask, what do the images symbolize</u>?

Cycle concept map

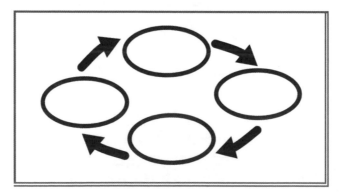

Language frame for cycle map (blank):

The first that happens is _____. After that _____. Then _____. Next is _____. And then the cycle repeats over again and again.

Cycle map for daily routine (non-academic)

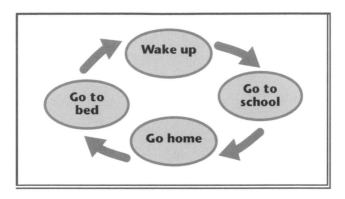

Note, this is the same content from the sequence map you saw above. Because it is repetitive it can become a cycle.

Language frame for daily routine cycle map (non-academic):

The first thing that happens <u>everyday is I wake up</u>. After that <u>I go to school</u>. Then <u>I go home</u>. Next <u>I go to bed</u>. And then the cycle repeats over and over again.

Cycle map for poverty cycle (academic):

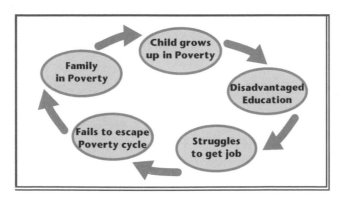

Note, this content should be familiar from the chapter 6: expert thinking.

Language frame for cycle map of the poverty cycle (academic):

When <u>you are born into a poor family</u> the first thing you do <u>is grow up poor</u>. After that <u>you get a disadvantaged education</u>. Then <u>you struggle to get a job</u>. Next you <u>fail to escape the poverty cycle</u>. And then <u>you stay in poverty</u>. And the cycle repeats itself over and over again.

Cause and effect concept map
The square in the middle is the event that occurred. The circles on the left are the antecedents. The corresponding circles on the right are the results of the event which occured.

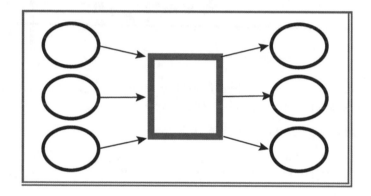

Language frame for cause and effect (blank):

There are _____ causes of _____ . The first _____ which resulted in _____. The second cause is _____ which resulted in _____. The third cause is _____ which resulted in _____.

Cause and effect map for why I get in trouble (non-academic):

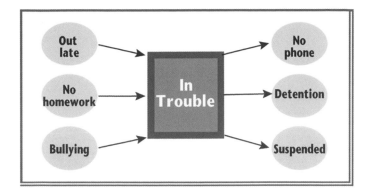

Language frame for why I get in trouble cause and effect map (non-academic):

There are <u>three</u> causes for <u>why I get into trouble</u>. The first is <u>staying out late</u> which results in <u>losing my phone privileges</u>. The second is <u>not doing my homework</u> which results in <u>getting detention</u> at school. The third is <u>bullying other students</u> which results <u>in getting suspended</u>.

Cause and effect for the scientific revolution (academic example):

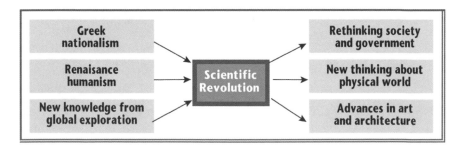

Language frame for scientific revolution cause and effect map (academic):

There were three causes of the <u>scientific revolution</u>. The first was <u>Greek rationalism</u> which resulted in <u>the rethinking of society and government</u>. The second cause <u>was the renaissance and humanism</u> which resulted in <u>new thinking about the physical world</u>. The third cause was <u>new knowledge from global exploration</u> which resulted in <u>advances in art and architecture</u>.

APPENDIX II
LEARNING PROGRESSION (INFLEXIBLE – FLEXIBLE – APPLICATION)

Application! Application! Application! The only word that has been uttered as many times in schools as application over the past decade is rigor! What these two terms have in common is the number and variety of their definitions. Regardless though, both application and rigor are laudable goals, and there is one curricular sequence best used to attain both. That sequence is Inflexible – Flexible – Application (you may sometimes see this learning progression described as Remember – Understand – Apply). In other words, first teaching knowledge and skills that are *inflexible*, then moving to knowledge and skills that are *flexible*, and finally knowledge and skills used in an *application*. Let's look at some examples.

First, a non-academic example. Imagine teaching a child to hit a baseball for the first time. You might begin by having them hit off of a batting tee: if the child has the same swing, on the same plane, she will hit the ball every time. This is an example of *inflexible* learning because if the child follows the same rules then she will hit the ball successfully every time.

After the child has become proficient, or near proficient, at hitting off the tee, you might begin to have the child attempt to hit some very slow controlled pitches. The task of hitting the ball has become *flexible* because the basics of swinging the bat are the same but the context has changed. The rules of how to hit the ball have altered slightly.

Finally, after practicing hitting slowly pitched balls it might be time to hit in a game. All the rules about hitting the ball, and still more to be learned, are needed to become successful. This is *application*.

The point is, we learn best from inflexible to flexible to application. If, as teachers, we move too fast to application many students will not be successful. It is better to go slow than to go fast.

Willingham (2000) describes the Inflexible – Flexible – Application progression in the following terms. Inflexible knowledge is neat but unsophisticated. For example, when first learning about metaphors what is being compared is clear and obvious. There is no question about the referent nor its qualities. In contrast, an extended metaphor is more flexible. There is still a referent, there are still qualities, but the two are not as explicit as in the first example. Only after students have understood a metaphor in an inflexible manner can they be expected to move to flexible learning such as extended metaphors. Application would be the use of metaphors in original writing.

Another example of progressing from inflexible to flexible is teaching students the simple past tense of verbs. The inflexible knowledge here is that in order to create the simple past tense of a verb you add the suffix 'ed' (e.g. to jump, jumped). The flexible knowledge is that some verbs are irregular (e.g. to run, ran; to swim, swam). The application would be using the proper form of the simple past tense in speaking and writing.

Warning! It is only after the students have progressed from inflexible to flexible that they are ready to be exposed to variations. Many publishers do not take this research into account when writing their textbooks. It is common that many variations are presented by a text in a single lesson. This is your classroom. Be the boss of the book, do not let the book be the boss of you!

APPENDIX III
CLASSROOM PROCEDURES

To *Teach FAST* there must be certain classroom procedures in place to keep lessons moving. If you lose a minute here, 30 seconds there, another 2 minutes over here, all of a sudden you have wasted a significant amount of time. Why is it significant? If you are teaching a primary grade then OWL 1 is only 5-7 minutes. If you lose your OWL you impact your guided practice. If you limit guided practice you have compromised formative data. If you have compromised the formative data then you are not making informed instructional decisions.

In order to avoid predictable delays here is a list of classroom procedures you should teach and practice with your students.

STUDENT PARTNERS
Make sure students have a partner before the lesson starts. It does not matter how you decide to partner students. Some teachers assign partners on an individual basis, others assign them by how the students are seated, or allow students to choose their partners, or assign 'shoulder partners', 'cross partners', etc. The key thing is to deal with this before the lesson starts. Also, have methods to determine which partner speaks first. This will eliminate hearing students say, 'You go first. No, you go first.'

How partners are assigned is irrelevant and who goes first is irrelevant. What is relevant is that when the teacher says, 'Point to your partner. Raise your hand if you are going first', there is no hesitation.

Practice these commands:

- Point to your partner.
- Raise your hand if you do not have a partner.
- The person sitting closer to the door is going first.
- Raise your hand if you are going first.

Or the person with the darker hair, or the person who … you get the idea. However, you determine who goes first, make sure it is fast.[169] Practice these commands repeatedly until your students know *exactly* what to do during a lesson.

Why is this important? More than 75% of the time students should be able to tell their partner whatever they need to tell them within 10 seconds. It doesn't make any sense to have students spend 30 seconds finding a partner that they will talk to for 5 seconds. Tick tock, tick tock.

PRACTICE USING LANGUAGE FRAMES
If you were teaching adults and told them you would be using a language frame then you would need to demonstrate that frame for them. If adults need something demonstrated, then there is a 100% chance children will need a demonstration as well.

Practice language frames when you first introduce them to students. Model any new language frames when using them with new content.

The purpose of the language frame is to alow student to focus on concepts. By design they are meant to be a little loose.[170] That means they are not meant to be structured to be grammatically correct in all circumstances. This looseness allows for slight variations of answers from students. However, this looseness can confuse some people. A quick demonstration will be all that is needed to resolve this. This is especially true if the use of language frames is part of the culture of the classroom.

---

169 I have seen teachers say, 'The taller partner goes first.' It sounds cute, but when students are getting up from their seats to stand back-to-back and asking other students to judge who is taller … well, tick tock, tick tock.

170 The younger the students, the less loose they should be. If you are using language frames with English Learners (EL) make sure that they are tight, e.g. there is verb subject agreement and they are grammatically correct, etc.

PRACTICE USING WHITEBOARDS

Practice using the mundane aspects of any technology that is to be used in instruction. Students should practice the distribution of devices, logging in, getting to frequently used platforms, etc.

Once, before a training, a teacher picked up one of the individual whiteboards that had been distributed to everyone, and disparagingly said, 'Look! A low-tech iPad.' White boards at every child's desk may be low-tech, but sometimes low-tech works pretty damn well. The purpose of every student having a white board is to allow the teacher to quickly and efficiently check for understanding, increasing student accountability. It allows teachers to deliver feedback to more students more efficiently.

All of these wonderful benefits only occur if the students use white boards as directed – so practice getting whiteboards, pens, and erasers to desks. There are several ways of doing this. Some teachers have students keep whiteboards, pens, and erasers at the their desks so that the students 'own' their own supplies. Other teachers have whiteboards and supplies in a central location and have students get out of their seats to retrieve the supplies. They use the time as a quick physiology bump by having students up and moving. Which ever method you decide to use be sure to practice. Become efficient.

Once, while I was observing a 3rd grade math lesson, the teacher directed the students to get their whiteboards, markers, and erasers out of their desk. Thinking that this was going to be a disastrous time suck, I looked at my watch to accurately record how much class time would be wasted. Eight seconds! It only took 3rd graders eight seconds to get their supplies out of their desks and be ready for guided practice. This shows the importance of practice. Every time you must wait for students to get their whiteboards and markers you should be hearing in your head, 'tick tock, tick tock.'

HOW TO HOLD WHITE BOARD UP

One of the biggest reasons white boards make checking for understanding efficient is that teachers can stand at the front of the class and see every students' work. This is only true if students hold their board up with two hands in the vicinity of their chins with the proper side facing the teacher. Why is this important? Every time during lesson you have to tell a student to hold his white board properly so you can see it is wasted time. Tick tock, tick tock.

TEACH STUDENTS TO RESPOND TO CHECKING FOR UNDERSTANDING QUESTIONS

Rules when responding to checking for understanding questions:

- Do not shout out.
- Do not raise hands.

Every time a student responds to a teacher's question, that student is recalling and relearning information stored in the brain. The student does not need to respond verbally to the teacher in order to recall that information. However, the student *does* need to mentally engage, without interruption or assistance such as from other students calling out answers. All students should have the opportunity to benefit from recalling information.

Often teachers call on the students who raise their hands first. When those students who have their hands up first are called on to respond, the other students are robbed of the opportunity to recall the information. That means that students who take just a few seconds longer to recall the information are robbed of the practice of recalling the information and lose the opportunity to make those neural connections that make learning permanent.

To remedy both issues tell the students you are about to ask a checking for understanding question. When you ask a checking for understanding question students are not to raise their hands. The students do not need to raise their hands because you will be calling on students 'randomly'.[171]

This is tough for primary teachers who are trying to teach their students to raise their hands before speaking. In order to reinforce this behavior teachers often call on students who raise their hands. If you are one of those teachers who are training your students not to shout out answers without being called upon you can try the following. Tell the students that

---

171 Please do not call on students randomly. It is a time waster. See 'canary students' below. Tick tock, tick tock.

you are going to ask a checking for understanding question. Tell them to think of their answer and sit quietly. After all the students have had time to think, *then* tell the students to raise their hands if they have an answer. You are still training students to raise their hands, and you are giving everyone an opportunity to recall and relearn the information.

WHEN ASKING CHECKING FOR UNDERSTANDING QUESTIONS

Do not call on individual students before you ask a question. This usually looks like this: 'Maria, can you tell the class what is in the First Amendment?' Once a teacher directs a question to a single student, the rest of the class take it as a cue to 'sit this one out.'[172]

Practice the procedure

Tell the students you are going to ask a checking for understanding question. Ask the students to tell their partner the rules for answering checking for understanding questions. Call on several students to repeat the answers.

Random students? Use canary students

The purpose of asking students checking for understanding questions is two-fold. The first reason is to give students the opportunity to recall and relearn content. The second reason is to collect data on how students are performing.

An efficient way to collect data is by calling on canary students.[173] The origin of the term comes from the proverbial 'canary in the coalmine.' Prior to high-tech gas sensors, miners used to bring canaries into the coal mines to judge the safety of the air in the mine. A canary's lungs are smaller than a human's. If the canary survived, the air was safe. If the canary perished … well, you know the rest.

---

172 If you happen to slip and find that you have called one student, you can easily recover. Remember, in the classroom there is nothing fatal, nothing final. If you catch yourself calling on someone just say, 'Instead of just Maria, I want all of you to think about what is in the First Amendment.'

173 I am not sure where this concept originated. I learned it from Dr. Frank Rodrigues.

In your class you have students who can serve as canary students. They are the students who inform you if it is safe to go forward with the lesson or if you need to slow down. Your canary students are not your top students who always understand the lesson. They are not the struggling students who consistently have a difficult time understanding. They are those who are in the middle: the students who sometimes understand and sometimes don't understand.

Canary students are super data carriers. If the canary students understand you can rest assured your top students understand. If the canary students do not get it, you can infer your struggling students may not get it either.

STUDENT BEHAVIOR DURING MODELING

Modeling is the only time during the lesson when students are not to engage in any conversation, ask questions, or comment. This is contrary to what many teachers have been taught about encouraging student engagement.

When delivering the lessons using the FAST Framework students are encouraged (commanded!) to participate and be actively engaged during all the lesson components except when the teacher is modeling. Students talk during the preview. Students talk during the lesson objective. Students talk during the review. Students talk during key ideas. Students talk during guided practice. Students talk during closure. Students *do not* talk during modeling.

If the lesson has been properly chunked, and if there are no interruptions, the students will be silent for no longer than 2-3 minutes.

Practice and remind students: NO INTERRUPTIONS! Successful training requires repetitions. Here are two of the most successful methods I have seen teachers use to teach and practice no talking during modeling – each requires reminders to students.[174]

    A. Prompt: 'When you go to the movies are you supposed to talk? Well I am the movie. No questions while I model. I will answer

---

174 As with all classroom procedures these need to be practiced and reinforced constantly.

any questions when I am done.' This eventually morphs into, 'I am going to model. What does that mean?'

B. Prompt: 'I am going to model now. Who would like to put our sign up?'

A student is selected to put a laminated sign similar to the below image on the whiteboard in the front of the room. The teacher calls on a student to explain what the sign means. All students then explain, 'No hands up during modeling.'

Remember, remind and check!

APPENDIX IV
DECLARATIVE AND PROCEDURAL LESSONS

Declarative lessons focus on learning a new concept, procedural lessons focus on learning a new skill. Although many similarities exist between procedural and declarative lessons, it is very helpful to identify your lesson as one or the other before beginning to design it.[175] Determining the type of lesson you will be teaching will limit the number of decisions to be made.

Both types of lessons are designed using the FAST Framework, but there are differences between the two in both design and delivery. Below is a table summarizing similarities and differences.

---

175 If during your planning you believe you could teach your learning objective either as a declarative lesson or a procedural lesson, choose procedural. It is always easier to have students perform a task using steps.

LESSON COMPONENT	PROCEDURAL	DECLARATIVE	SAME/DIFFERENT
Preview Goal: Students access prior conceptual knowledge	**Design:** Questions for all students. Do not need to be based on academic experience. **Delivery:** Ask questions to prompt student memory	**Design:** Questions for all students. Do not need to be based on academic experience. **Delivery:** Ask questions to prompt student memory	Same
Learning Objective Goal: Single Focus	**Design:** Matches Ind Practice **Delivery:** Written and visible to students	**Design:** Matches Ind Practice **Delivery:** Written and visible to students	Same
Review Goal: Recall/practice prior skill	**Design:** Teacher identities constituent skills in procedure. **Delivery:** Students asked to perform tasks	**Design:** Teacher identifies skills needed to perform Learning Objective **Delivery:** May not be necessary.	Different
Key Ideas Goal: Present declarative and conditional concepts	**Design:** Concept may be new. **Delivery:** Use concept maps and language frames. Demand students use language frames.	**Design:** Concept is always new. **Delivery:** Use concept maps and language frames. Demand students use language frames	Same
Expert Thinking Goal: Provide a model	**Design:** Steps to show how teacher performs **Delivery:** Teacher performs tasks, solves problems, etc., using steps. First person to explain her thinking. "When I solve a problem like this, the first thing I do is ..."	**Design:** Concept maps to visually demonstrate how the teacher relates ideas, **Delivery:** First person. e.g., "When I think about the impact of gentrification on poverty ..."	Different: Presentation of Key Ideas and Expert Thinking are distinct and separate in Procedural Lesson. In Declarative Lessons the components become integrated
Guided Practice (Gradual Release) Goal: Facilitate immediate student practice	**Design:** Practice is exactly the same as Ind Practice. **Delivery:** Gradual release using steps	**Design:** Practice approximates Independent Practice. **Delivery:** Cognitive demand increases by facilitating activities	Different: Procedural Lesson Guided Practice is exactly the same as what is modeled. Declarative lessons provide opportunities to interact intellectually with content in different contexts.
Closure Goal: Final Check for Understanding (Collect formative data)	**Design:** Questions from three components of the lesson: LO, Key Ideas, Expert Thinking **Delivery:** Teacher asks, students perform	**Design:** Questions from three components of the lesson: LO, Key Ideas, Expert Thinking **Delivery:** Teacher asks, students perform	Same
Independent Practice Goal: Immediate student practice repetitions	**Design:** Ind Practice is exactly the same as the guided practice **Delivery:** Students who are able begin Ind Practice; other students receive immediate in-class intervention.	**Design:** Ind Practice incorporates knowledge/understanding in a new context **Delivery:** Students who are able begin Independent Practice; other students receive immediate in-class intervention.	Same

Both procedural and declarative lessons are similar up until the point in a procedural lesson when the teacher begins to model the procedure. Both lesson types use a concept map. Both use a language frame.

Procedural lessons have a gradual release of control from the teacher to the students during guided practice. Declarative lessons do this through an increasing degree of cognitive engagement beginning with the preview.

Both procedural and declarative lessons always have a concept. In procedural lessons the concept *may* be new, but the skill, procedure, is *always* new. In declarative lessons the concept is *always* new, but the skill is *never* new.

ACKNOWLEDGMENTS

No worthwhile endeavor is ever accomplished alone. For me, the completion of *Teach FAST* was one of those worthwhile and meaningful endeavors. With that in mind, I must acknowledge some special people and their contributions to this project.

First, my wife Denise who provided just the support I needed by believing I could finish but never directly asking or commenting about it. Never once did she wonder out loud, 'You say you are working on a book. Where is it?' Thank you for giving me the space I needed.

My mentor and partner Dr. Randall Olson, for his continuing support in not just this enterprise but throughout my career. I am sure many times he thought the best advice he could give me was to continue taking my meds.

To the individuals who over the years worked on creating the FAST Framework and making it the sophisticated structure it has become: Carin Contreras, Dr. Frank Rodrigues, and Dr. Janae Tovar. Each brought expertise and intellectual honesty to discussions about instruction.

A big thank you to my long-time friend Carl Twisselman who brought his creative talents to the project that kept me motivated.

And finally, to all the terrific teachers and educators with whom I have worked for the past 20 years. I know it is cliché, but I really did learn so much from those teachers who took the ideas that are presented in this book, made them their own, and made them better.